FROM TIPI TO SKYSCRAPER

A HISTORY OF WOMEN IN ARCHITECTURE

BY DORIS COLE

Photo Credits

Browne and Nichols School Collection: page 73
California Department of Parks and Recreation: page 113
Chicago Historical Society: pages 58, 116–117
William and Henry Frost Collection: pages 79, 84–85, 86, 91, 92, 97
Fruitlands Museum, Harvard, Massachusetts: pages 62–63, 66, 68–69, 71
The Kansas Historical Society: pages 12, 13, 24, 30–31
Department of Photography, Ohio State University: page 106
Peabody Museum, Harvard University: pages xiv, 4, 6–7, 10–11, 15, 16, 18–19, 21, 23
Public Housing Administration, Nursing and Home Finance Agency: page 109
Schlesinger Library, Radcliffe College: pages 35, 38, 40, 42, 43, 44, 45, 46–47

Book design by Robbie Pfeufer

i press incorporated
145 Hanover Street
Boston, Mass. 02108

Distributed by George Braziller
One Park Avenue
New York, N.Y. 10016

Library of Congress Catalog Number: 73-80932
ISBN: cloth 0-913222-01-1
       paper 0-913222-02-X

Contents

Preface and Acknowledgement

This history of women in architecture is intended to be only a first step in documenting and studying women's contributions to architecture. Through the process of developing this book I have been able to answer some of my own questions, and questions asked by others, concerning women architects. Most important, it has made me aware of how much more there is to know about women in architecture.

In this initial study I have purposely dealt with trends rather than with the practices of individuals, though there are many women architects whose work should be documented. Practically none of my information comes from conventional architectural books; women are rarely mentioned in such books. I wrote to many women architects. Some did and some did not answer my letter, and one was violently opposed to such a study. It was never my intent, however, to speak for all women architects.

The photographs included in this book illustrate general trends discussed in the text; they were not selected to present the work of individual women architects. The photographs cover the period from 1800 through World War II. I have not shown more recent projects because, despite the fact that at times their work is singled out in professional journals, women architects today are still in transition from domestic to civic architecture, from draftswomen to decision formulators within the corporate firm. Since their participation is neither independent nor equal and their potential not yet fully developed, this was best illustrated through omission.

Though this book can be linked to the contemporary women's movement, my objective in writing it was documentary rather than ideological; hopefully the material presented here can help broaden the understanding of American architecture in general.

I must thank the people who encouraged me — and discouraged me — in this project, for they all spurred me on in my work. Though only a few are listed below, I am indebted to many people and institutions for their help.

Sergio Berizzi, Architect
Mary Otis Stevens, Architect
Dr. Janice Cole
Mr. and Mrs. Louis Cole

Smith College Archives, Northampton, Massachusetts
Schlesinger Library, Radcliffe College
Boston Public Library

All the women architects who very kindly answered questions, sent information, and expressed their thoughts with candor and wit.

Doris Cole was born in Chicago, Illinois, and grew up in Grand Rapids, Michigan. Graduating in 1959 cum laude from Radcliffe College, she received her Master of Architecture degree from Harvard Graduate School of Design. The author is married to the architect Sergio Berizzi, and lives in Concord, Massachusetts. In 1965-66 she was a Visiting Critic in the Department of Architecture at the Rhode Island School of Design, and in 1973 was appointed to the AIA National Committee on correctional architecture. She is a registered architect and is certified by the National Council of Architectural Registration Boards.

Introduction

This study will, first, document the historic contributions of women to American architecture; second, analyze the underlying social and economic reasons for the present situation; and third, propose ways of correcting and improving this situation by attracting more women to the profession of architecture. This book is part of the general discussion concerning women in this country; it is part of a trend and, hopefully, this trend will lead not only to further discussion but to constructive activity. One cannot deny the facts, but perhaps many people will disagree with the point of view expressed in this book. The ideas presented here are based upon research, interviews, and discussions with my male and female colleagues and, not surprisingly, there was a diversity of opinions, ideas, and goals, even among the women. The point is not that women are more likely than their male counterparts to have found the answers to the difficult issues confronting the profession of architecture, but that perhaps they are raising some new and different questions which are pertinent to its future.

Approximately 2 percent of the architects practicing today are women. Less than one half of the women who have earned architectural degrees are registered architects. Though the number of women earning these degrees is increasing, the percentage of degrees granted to women is decreasing as the profession grows. Why is this happening? Is opportunity or inclination lacking? Though today's statistics are not promising, the dearth of women in architecture cannot be considered a natural state, since it did not exist throughout the history of our country.

Women in the United States have been active, influential participants in developing and formulating America's architecture. Historically, women have been major collaborators, if not prime instigators, in this field. From the raising of the tipi to frontier blazing to the Utopian communes of the Shakers to the nineteenth-century concerned client and her carpenter, women have dealt with civil and domestic architecture. Although — and perhaps because — they have rarely been part of the organized profession, women have used their architectural skills indirectly toward improving the social, physical, and moral character of their families and nation.

The architectural profession today is often romanticized or scorned. Architects are called "form-makers" and "master builders," enhancing the prestige of rich private clients and corporations. Perhaps this description exaggerates the situation, but the profession itself admits that it is not adequately serving our society's broad base. Women have addressed themselves to the daily, ordinary problems of living through their connection with architecture. In fact, their interest in it has often been motivated by their very concern over cultural and social deficiencies in American life. Traditionally, it was the women who addressed themselves to social architecture, while professional organizations like the American Institute of Architects are just now beginning to focus upon this whole area of responsibility. It would be advantageous for the development of the profession — and the nation — to have a more significant collaboration in contemporary architecture between men and women, and thereby gain the experience of these women in social architecture. By working together, as men and women did when founding this nation, our chances of developing appropriate architectural solutions for America's current social needs will improve significantly.

In a study like this one, it is always interesting to draw parallels between America and other nations, to investigate women in the European countries, in new nations such as Israel, and in the revolutionary societies of Russia and China, and to understand what role women have played in the development of their respective architectures. Some statistics can be found, and they are quite contrary to accepted beliefs. For example, in 1969, 18 percent of the registered architects in Milan were women, which is typical in Italy and certainly much higher than in the United States. But such statistics must be interpreted in terms of the social and class structure, economic pressures, and political realities which affect the nations and the women who function within them. We cannot make contemporary comparisons until we clarify the historic growth patterns within each country. It is a tremendous task, and far beyond the scope of this initial study of women in architecture.

Although similarities, of course, exist among nations, the problems, historic patterns, and future potential of American women are unique to this country, and founded upon the unique attributes of our nation. American women, and women architects, can look to other nations for suggestions, but it is within the confines and structure of their own society that they must find their place. It is with that conviction in mind that I attempted to compile the first history of women in American architecture.

A HISTORY OF WOMEN IN ARCHITECTURE

Ute Indians on western slope of Wasatch Mountains, Utah.

1 FRONTIER TRADITIONS

Pioneers and Indians

It was on the plain of survival rather than on any mythological frontier that the American pioneers came face to face with the American Indians. Though their goals were often different, their lives and problems were far more similar than the white settler wished to admit. The pioneers were new to this land and ignorant of its problems and, because of this, they often failed in their struggle to survive. The Indians, on the other hand, were ancient inhabitants and had already learned how to survive successfully; they were at the apex of their knowledge. It was from the Indians that the pioneers learned their method of living and much of their architecture.

The frontier began with the first settlers spreading up and down the Atlantic coast, but as more settlers arrived they pushed west to the Mississippi and, soon, beyond. This expansion continued well into the 1890s, until there was no further place to go. There was no territory left for the pioneer who wished to find the promise of Eden, for the misfit or loner who wished to wander in the wilderness, for the unsuccessful who sought success in the open land. The closing of the frontier also meant that there was no territory left for the Indian. Both the Indian and pioneer had looked to the frontier for a type of life which only this wilderness could provide and support. It was basically a nomadic and rural life, with all of its concomitant problems and hardships. This life-style was valued and shared by pioneer and Indian alike, and it continued until the spreading urbanization of America destroyed them both.

Life was extremely difficult in this land, and the pioneer developed a devotion to hard work and a distrust for idle leisure. There was no place for people, male or female, Indian or pioneer, who did not share in the work. Meeting the demands of the environment and the necessary labor to sustain life influenced the status of women

1

among both the pioneers and the Indians. A woman was valued for her ability to contribute. The pioneer woman "built the fires, milked the cows, cared for a kitchen garden, fetched wood and water, cooked meals, churned butter, spun flax, wove cloth, and fashioned clothes for the entire family."[1] The Indian woman did essentially the same things for her family and community. In both the Indian and pioneer cultures women were active contributors; the conditions of existence were too marginal to support any idle group.

Yet from hard work came honor and respect. Among the Iroquois Confederacy, one of the strongest and most powerful Indian groups of the Northeast, women had a position of considerable importance. Although they did not participate in the council meetings, they had the power to veto a council decision. The Iroquois woman owned the house and all household possessions; the man could claim only his tools, weapons, and the clothing which he wore. Descent was determined through the mother rather than the father, and both women and men had the right to divorce.

This status of women was not confined solely to the Iroquois Confederacy. Among the Hopi Indians, women also owned the houses, headed the households, and had equal rights to divorce. So, too, ownership of the house and household equipment went to the women among the Indian tribes of the Great Plains. But one must never forget when speaking of the status of Indian women that they were not an idle group supported by their men. In *Daughters of the Country*, Walter O'Meara carefully explained that "as in most other aspects of Indian life a woman's status varied from one tribe to another. Much depended on her importance in the economy."[2]

The Indian women were the architects of their communities. Among many Indian tribes of North America, the women designed, fabricated, and constructed the dwelling units. In fact, architecture was often considered women's work. "As in all primitive societies, the male accepted those tasks calling for relatively short bursts of energy, muscular exertion, and exposure to danger, while the woman performed routine work demanding patience, endurance, and manual skill."[3] It was "patience, endurance, and manual skill" which were required in developing suitable structures for the life of the North American Indians. The Indian women held this knowledge, and it was from them that the European adventurers had to learn if they

2

were to survive the hardships of the frontier. While the pioneer woman was beginning her apprenticeship in architecture, the Indian woman was at the peak of her career.

The architecture of the Indians was as varied as the landscape of North America. In the frozen North there was the Eskimo with the winter igloo made of snow blocks or logs and the summer tent made from skins. In the forests of the Northwest the architecture was, most naturally, of wood, with houses of split planks and dormer roofs. In the forests of the Northeast the houses were also made from wood, using bent boughs to form the framework covered with mats in the winter and bark sheathing in the summer. In the southwest of Arizona and New Mexico, semiarid and with little lumber available, the architectural solution was the pueblo, made from small stones, and the mud adobe. At the edge of the Great Plains there were the pit houses — actual pits dug into the earth with light structures above to serve as roofs. At a later date, with the coming of the railroad, even railroad ties were used by the Navaho Indians and developed into the architecture of the "hogan," an eight-sided wooden building, open to the east, with a roof similar to the pit house but constructed on ground level.[4] And on the Great Plains, where the brave nomadic Indians roamed hunting the huge buffalo, the architectural solution was the tipi. Perhaps because of its efficiency and versatility as a shelter, the tipi was the most elegant architectural solution of them all.

As can be seen from these examples, the architecture of the North American Indians was indeed varied. It was not varied due to whim, but represented the adaptation of a tribal life-style to the amenities and limitations of a given physical environment. The Indian precedents were lessons from which the first European settlers learned: those who survived learned their lessons well and reflected the varied architecture of the Indians in their own architectural innovations.

In those Indian tribes where women were not primarily responsible for constructing dwellings, they were still often responsible for related arts and crafts. For example, among the Indians of the Northwest, descent was through the men, and the men owned the houses. In this culture, wealth was determined by the number of beautiful blankets owned by the men, and the women's task was to weave these blankets. It is interesting to note, however, that men

designed the blankets and their "heraldic designs," showing through symbol the power and glories of their owners, while women provided the needed labor for weaving these designs into blankets. Evidently it was common among these Northwest Indian tribes that men designed, and often fabricated, items that held profound spiritual or totemic meanings, while women designed and fabricated those items that were of practical use for maintaining the life of the community. For instance, when it came to the geometric designs for the mats and baskets, women were the designers as well as the skilled laborers. The mats and baskets were not indications of wealth and influence, nor were they endowed with spiritual meaning. These were everyday household items made and used by women.

It was in the Southwest and on the Great Plains that women were most active in formulating and constructing the dwellings; among these many tribes women owned, designed, and produced the houses with their own labor. The Indians of the Great Plains — Comanche, Kiowa, Cheyenne, Arapaho, Blackfoot, Sioux, Arikara, Mandan, Hidatsa, Crow, Pawnee — are well known to our contemporary society: the buffalo hunt, the brave warriors, and the ever-present tipi are legendary. Though often distorted and misunderstood, few dwellings in all the world have provoked the imagination like the tipi of the Plains Indians. Unfortunately, many have neglected to mention that it was the Indian woman who was responsible for the tipi. "She tanned the hides and from them fashioned lodge covers. She made the tipi, set it up, and took it down when the encampment moved on."[5]

A tipi was not only beautiful but practical, being one of the most efficient shelters for a migrant people. This efficiency was well recognized by Kit Carson, who insisted upon using a tipi when accompanying Lieutenant John Charles Fremont on his first exploratory expedition. In their history of the tipi, Reginald and Gladys Laubin observe that "other tents are hard to pitch, hot in summer, cold in winter, badly lighted, unventilated, easily blown down, and ugly to boot. The conical tent of the Plains Indians has none of these faults. It can be pitched if necessary, by a single person. It is roomy, well ventilated at all times, cool in summer, well lighted, proof against high winds and heavy downpours, and, with its cheerful inside fire, snug in the severest winter weather."[6] Such a superb structure, which looks so "simple," was achieved only through great subtlety of design and

General Brook's Camp near Pine Ridge, South Dakota. January 17, 1891.

generations of experience. The utility of the tipi was recognized by others beside Kit Carson and the early explorers of the Great Plains and the new West. It was ironical to find that the United States soldiers who finally defeated the Indians actually used tents based upon the design of the Indian tipi. The architectural form which had for so long protected the Indians, had given them shelter and comfort, was used against them.

The name of the person who designed the first tipi is unknown, and, in fact, it would probably be impossible to assign credit to a single individual. The design of the tipi in its present form developed through an unknown length of time, being adapted to changing conditions in the tribal community. The design and fabrication of these tipis was always communal, with many people working on each structure and leaving the mark of their craftsmanship and ideas.

The development of the tipi can be divided into three stages: 1. the bark and brush tipi used before the Indian tribes migrated to the Great Plains; 2. the skin tipi used while the Indians hunted the buffalo on the Great Plains; and 3. the canvas-covered tipi used when the buffalo was gone and the Indians no longer controlled their own territory. The design of the tipi reached its culmination during the buffalo-hunting period, the canvas tipi being a copy of this form. The tipi consisted of poles, exterior lodge cover with smoke flaps, interior lining, ground cloths, drainage trench, stone circle, parfleches, bags, and pillows.

While the men provided the raw material by hunting the buffalo, the women designed, fabricated, erected, and owned the tipis. With careful construction and subtle design, these Indian women were able to create comfortable villages for their communities. Though severely limited in their building materials, the architects produced dwellings that were not only remarkably comfortable but were adapted to their migrant lives. "We are convinced that Indians, in their buffalo-hide tipis, with plenty of warm furs and robes, were far more comfortable than the pioneers in their log cabins, heated with one fireplace only."[7] Unfortunately for the pioneers, they did not take up the tipi as a building form for their own homes. The reason may be that the settlers, even though often transient, did not consider themselves migrants and so did not adopt the tipi, which was designed primarily for the migratory life.

The development of the tipi as an architectural form was also dependent upon the abundance and hunting of buffalo. Though many of the early frontiersmen hunted buffalo, this was not the usual occupation for pioneer family men. Hunting buffalo did, however, become dominant in the culture of the Great Plains Indians. As the Indians went west, more and more of the tribes were transformed into primarily hunting and migrant people. Buffalo herds were there to be hunted, and their valuable hides and meat not only brought prosperity to the Indians but changed many of their native crafts. Before the days of the great buffalo hunts, tipis were often covered with sheets of bark. The extensive use of buffalo hides progressed as the Indian economy became increasingly dependent upon the buffalo. The hides were used for lodge covers, clothing, cooking pots, storage bags and boxes, pillows, and furniture. By the middle of the 1700s, pottery and baskets were replaced with rawhide containers, and even weaving cloth was abandoned in favor of soft, tanned skin for clothing. The women used and re-used practically every part of these enormous animals to shelter, clothe, and feed the Indian communities.

The Indian woman was not only in charge of the tipi and its interior; she was also responsible for choosing the location of village camp sites. Often near streams where water was available, the same sites were used over and over again — certainly testimony to the good site selection made by these women. There was no rigid geometrical or abstract plan for the usual Indian village of the Great Plains. The one rule followed was to have the tipis facing east, but this was for practical, not abstract, reasons, since on the plains the prevailing winds are westerly. An irregular plan was used in most of the villages of the Plains Indians, with each tipi located where the women of the household found it most convenient to camp. The one time when this irregular pattern was not used, however, was at the gathering for the summer Sun Dance. On these occasions, the tipis formed a large circle with each door facing towards the Sun Dance lodge. At times these encampments were very large, consisting of several circles each of which opened to the east. Aside from the practical reason, east, the direction of the sun, represented life and power to these people.

This one architectural form, the conical tipi, was adapted to the various functions of Indian village life. The tipi was most often used as the house or dwelling for the extended family, which consisted of the man, his first wife, her sisters (often taken as wives when their husbands died), and their children. The tipi was also used for the Chief's house; his tipi was usually larger, but not necessarily more

Crow Indian camp site at Little Big Horn River, Montana. 1870.

elaborate, than the others. The Warrior Society had its large tipi, but it was unfurnished, which made it necessary to borrow furnishings for the meetings. In the summer, kitchen tipis were set up; these kitchens were old tipis with the bottom cut off for greater ventilation. This same architectural form was used by the powerful and distinguished families of the tribes for their "medicine" tipis, intended to bring success and good fortune to the owners. The "medicine" tipi was painted with symbolic designs and was the only type of tipi which the Indians painted. However, "painting a tipi was usually man's work, and certain individuals specialized in it."[8] Again, the conical tipi was adapted to serve the functions of the Council Lodge. Since the Council meeting was attended by many people, it required one very large tipi, or a combination of two tipis to form one large central space. At death, the tipi was used as the burial lodge — and so demonstrated its versatility as an architectural form by serving ritual and social functions of the Plains Indians from the cradle to the grave.

Dodge City about 1875.

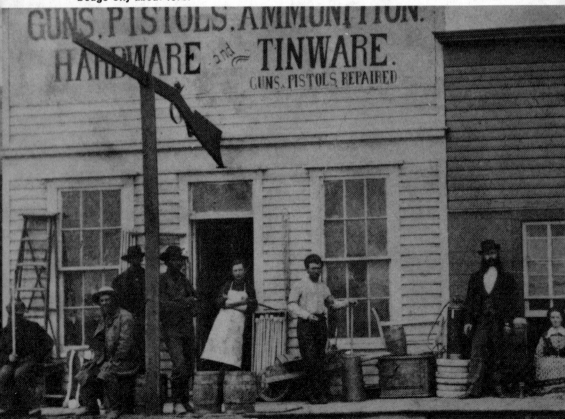

Moving day for the 100 foot long Lodge Hall in Bentley, Kansas, circa 1880.

In the same spirit the restless pioneer had begun to develop the movable lightweight dwelling. Though the tipi was not adopted as a permanent housing type by the American settlers, the principles of its design were appreciated. The tipi was a light frame of wood, consisting of three or four main poles tied together which could be lifted into place by one woman; on this light framework was put the outer skin of bark or buffalo. The settlers improvised light wood-frame constructions, drawing upon the example of the Indian tipi and their own previous knowledge of wood structures. The balloon frame and platform frame construction consisted of thin "poles" covered by thin wood sheathing, reflecting both the model of the tipi and similar environmental limitations shared by the Plains Indians. In other ways, too, the tipi and pioneer structures resembled each other. The tipi could be erected quickly, and so could the settlers' towns which began springing up practically overnight. The tipi could be dismantled and moved with little effort. The new pioneer towns also grew, shrunk, or changed. Mrs. Frances Trollope, an English traveler in 1831, reported with amazement that "one of the sights to stare at in America is that of houses moving from place to place."[9]

As the American settlers pushed west, as the railroad crossed the nation, and, most important, as the buffalo were exterminated, the Plains Indians lost the economic base of their society. The buffalo was the mainstay of the economy; the Plains Indian man was trained to hunt and was specialized in this skill; perhaps for this reason he could not adapt successfully to new circumstances. However, for the women, the architects, this challenge was met in an innovative manner. As buffalo became more scarce and contact with the traders more frequent, they adapted their architectural form to the material that was becoming available — canvas. Sturdy tipis could be made from canvas as well as from buffalo hides. Canvas was strong, lighter than hides, and could be purchased at the trading posts. Although women went on constructing their tipis and caring for their households, unfortunately "the destruction of the buffalo left in its wake total demoralization. Men's jobs were gone, and the men, untrained for any work but hunting, were left idle."[10]

The Plains Indian lost practically everything. They lost their land, their buffalo, their prosperity, their freedom, and often their lives. Despite all this, their architecture has survived and has been copied, admired, and glorified.

In the Southwest between the Colorado and Rio Grande Rivers, there is the Hopi Indian village of Old Oraibi, the oldest continuously used settlement in our country. It is a living part of the great tradition of both historic and prehistoric pueblo architecture found in this area of the United States. Its architecture is much admired by the professionals today and has been favorably compared by the architectural historian Vincent Scully to the Medieval Italian hill towns. The prehistoric ruins are described as "an almost delirious rhythm of rectangle and circle, of dwelling room and kiva."[11]

The great prehistoric pueblos were probably built between 700 and 1100 A.D., but their architecture has continued on as a viable form through the centuries. The historical Hopi village was usually divided into moieties, or halves; within the moieties were the clans, with descent through the women, who also owned both the houses and crops. The household consisted of a woman, her daughters, and their children. Husbands lived in their wives' houses but could be asked to leave and, if they left, would return to their mothers' homes. The clan was extremely important to the organization of the village and its ever-present religious ceremonies. For each clan in the village

Plaza at Oraibi Pueblo. Photo taken by A. C. Vroman in 1899.

Interior of Hopi Indian pueblo at Oraibi, Arizona. 1904.

there was a main home where the head woman usually lived and ritual objects for the clan were kept. The clans had their distinct religious functions and, although many more of the religious functions were carried out by the men than by the women, all members of the clans received their authority through matrilineal descent.

While the men farmed the fields and wove cloth, the women's duties were "to grind corn, to cook, to take care of babies, to plaster and repair houses, and to make baskets, plaques and pottery."[12] From childhood the women were trained in these skills. The woman ran the household with the help of her oldest brother, and she built this home with the help of her husband and brother.

Since the women helped to build the historic Pueblo villages, it is not unlikely that their female ancestors helped to construct the prehistoric Pueblo villages. The Hopi legends link themselves to the builders of the fantastically impressive and beautiful prehistoric villages built in the caves and on the cliffs of the Southwest. These remarkable towns were believed to have been built by "co-operating groups of moderately skilled individual men and, probably, women."[13]

The Pueblo Indian was a farmer, not a roaming hunter, and so did not need the portable dwellings found among the Indians of the Great Plains. Fixed in location, the Pueblo village needed on that account a site which could easily be defended. Therefore, many of the villages were located on high mesas or hills that provided natural defense against attack. The clans lived close together in these multi-leveled towns, with the men going out each day to work the fields.

In this semiarid land of the Hopis there was little wood for dwelling construction. When possible, small, flat stone slabs were used as a building material, and were so neatly laid up in ancient times that mortar was unnecessary to bind the walls. In other Pueblo villages, adobe was customarily used, with or without stones. Before the arrival of the Spanish, the builders constructed the walls in layers, putting the wet adobe on the dried mass and letting that layer dry before adding another. The Spanish introduced the pre-made, sun-dried adobe brick which was unknown to the Indians, thereby modifying the building material — but not the architectural form — of the pueblos. The building method included thin wood logs or poles on top of the stone or adobe walls, then brush on top of this substructure, and finally a layer of adobe to finish the flat roof. This type of construction was used both for dwellings and for the sacred kivas where the religious ceremonies took place.

Snake Dance Ceremony at Walpi Pueblo. Photo taken by A. C. Vroman 1899.

The dwelling for the extended matrilineal family was represented in religious symbolism as the worldly house where a person's spirit lived. In the Soyal ceremony seven songs blessed and described the seven stages of its construction — foundation, walls, beams and roof, plastering, niche, wood sticks for hanging articles, and fireplace. As the need arose through generations, the house was modified and enlarged with new rooms. Accordingly, the total structure grew in an irregular pattern. Each new builder added to the basic structure, suiting her own ideas and taste but guided by the traditions of her ancestors.

The rooms had flat roofs, and they were not without use. During the public dances in the central plaza, the people gathered on these terraces to view the ceremonies. In fact, during the dances for Wuwuchim, no one was permitted to be at plaza level, and the only place for viewing the ceremony was from the roofs. The flat roofs also provided access to the upper apartments and rooms. Beyond this, the flat terraced roofs transformed the entire small village into an amphitheater about the central plaza, the focus of the society's religious life.

The women and men who built these pueblos were the first town planners of North America. Much has changed and been lost through the centuries, but Old Oraibi has survived, not yet a ruins. In fact, it is still being occupied by Hopi family clans. Moreover, all three invaders — the Navajos, the Spanish, the pioneer Americans — were influenced by this Pueblo architecture. The stone and adobe construction pervasive in the Southwest was wisely imitated by the new settlers. "In any part of the country where moisture is excessive, this Pueblo type of architecture would not be satisfactory, but here it is eminently successful, as witness its long survival and its adoption as the basis for modern Southwestern architecture."[14]

Like the Pueblo Indians, the pioneers who settled the Southwest became farmers. The similarity of occupation, the common environmental conditions that they confronted, made it not surprising that the Pueblo style of architecture could be adopted almost directly by the pioneers. They saw the Indians building their homes of adobe, and they learned and improved upon the methods when they constructed their new forts, churches, missions, and farmhouses. Actually, there was little choice for the settlers but to follow the example of the Indians. With practically no lumber available, mud

San Miguel, the oldest church in Santa Fe, New Mexico.

adobe was the logical choice for the transplanted European trying to homestead an alien land. Combining Pueblo architecture with their native European traditions, the pioneers developed what is known as "Spanish mission style" with its thick, cooling walls and verandas.

Often it was the Indians themselves who constructed the churches, missions, and houses for the early European invaders, but their labor was rarely voluntary. The Spanish missionaries arriving in the 1600s forced Indian men and women to construct their buildings. These invaders sold their Indian captives as slaves to European families; the women went to single men who wanted wives. It was through such cruel and unhappy relationships between conqueror and conquered that the architectural knowledge of the Southwest Indians spread, beginning with the first Spanish invaders, who rarely brought European women with them, and continuing as a practice later by the homesteaders. Indian labor, first slave then hired help, built and maintained the settlers' homes. The Indian and pioneer were not friends, nor did their lives meet in co-operation, but in spite of this — and to the benefit of the pioneers — the architectural knowledge of the Hopi Indians and neighboring tribes was passed on. When the invaders captured the Indians, they captured a little of the Indian knowledge and were wise enough to recognize its value and adapt the Pueblo architectural tradition to their own needs.

As shown through the various Indian tribes of North America, the Indian woman did much more than tend to her children and family; she worked with her men to form their nations. Together the men and women built the igloos of the far North, produced the blankets of the Northwest, formed the Pueblo architecture of the Southwest and, with the buffalo skins provided by her men, the Indian woman made the tipis of the Great Plains. She was often honored in her tribe, and often owned the economic base of her community. If she was a force within her community, it was because she shared equally with the men the hard labor necessary to sustain their communal life, a life marked by the constant need to adapt to changing environmental conditions. As expressed in their diverse architectural traditions, North American Indian tribes possessed a sense of reality, variety, and an inventiveness of response to tribal needs and natural settings that were not matched, though often copied or adapted, by successive waves of European settlers.

The role of women in architecture was far more highly developed among the Indians than among the pioneers. The pioneer women worked extremely hard trying to bring some note of civilization to their homes and communities, but the Great Plains Indian women were able to go far beyond this. Architecture was solely their domain. The Indian women did everything from selecting the poles to butchering the buffalo to erecting the tipi. The Indian women of the Great Plains learned their architecture and construction skills from their mothers and other women. Even as little girls they made small tipis which they used to play house or to make homes for their favorite dogs. The making of a new lodge cover was a festive and communal event. When a woman needed a new lodge cover, she prepared a large feast and invited other women to come and join her for eating and working. The Indian women were proud of their skills and labor, keeping count of their tanned skins as carefully as the men kept count of their enemies' scalps. The men of the Plains Indians, though warriors and hunters who provided the essential buffalo hides, did not know how to make or construct tipis, nor did they know how to tan skins. These skills were solely known by the Indian woman, and she was proud of them.

The role played by women in architecture among the settlers was much more limited. Pioneer women were aware of the needs and tried to impose their will, but their architectural skills were only partially appreciated by the men in their communities. As the 1800s progressed, women began to write more and more handbooks on architecture. Though published mainly in the East, these handbooks were extremely popular throughout the country. In fact, the Western literary market was so important that publishing schedules were geared to seasonal weather which governed the opening and closing of the westward trails. *Letters to Young Ladies* (1833), *The Young Lady's Friend* (1837), *The Young Lady's Home* (1839), *Woman In Her Various Relations* (1853), *Manners* (1866), and *The American Woman's Home* (1869) were just a few of the books and magazines which served as architectural handbooks back and forth across this country.

The early pioneer women, though never drawing parallels between themselves and Indians, shared many conditions in common trying to provide comfortable and healthful homes and communities.

Dodge City's Front Street, September 1872.

Like their Indian women contemporaries, these early pioneer women shared equally with their men the daily frustrations, hard work, and problems of survival, but as time passed the female descendants of the pioneers were increasingly restricted in their scope of action. As the frontier closed, their "proper" social role was confined to the home and church. The architectural handbooks reflect this narrowing domain for women and show with this growing isolation that the descendants of the pioneer woman did not fully develop her architectural skills and never reached the North American Indian woman's level of participation in society.

As previously noted, part of the Indian woman's success in developing her architecture was the inclination toward and emphasis upon usable design. It was common among the Indian tribes that men designed, and often fabricated, items that held profound spiritual or totemic meanings, while the women designed and fabricated those items, including dwellings, that were of direct use in maintaining the life of the community. "This type of design division was usual throughout North America."[15] While the women characteristically used their skills to sustain tribal life rather than to glorify the gods and spirits, Indian men generally directed ceremonial and symbolic events. The main religious ceremonies of the Pueblo Indians were left to men; the symbolic decorations on the "medicine" tipis of the Great Plains Indians were done by men; the "heraldic" designs on the blankets of the Northwest were also by men. The women designed and fabricated the essential artifacts of daily life, concerning themselves with utility rather than abstractions.

Lessons in form, content, and method were what the Indian architects presented to the pioneers and their descendants. Jeannettee Henry Costo, editor of The Indian Historian Press, wrote that "we usually consider [Indian] dwellings, religious structures, gate ring centers, and temporary shelters, exactly as such. It might also be considered the beginning of a type of architecture centrally tied to the way of life, the environment and the earth. These varied with climate, geographical location, the form of the society, and the relationships of clans and families."[16] Some of these lessons were learned by the early settlers, but many of the principles, particularly those having to do with ecological adaptation to and use of the environment, are still to be appreciated and developed. A devotion to social architecture, a respect for environmental realities, and an appreciation for functional requirements are not yet characteristic of the architectural profession.

Crow Indian decorating rawhide. December 24, 1904.

Both in their architecture and daily life routines, the Indians and early pioneers had in common the practice of men and women working closely together and sharing work, responsibilities, and honor equally. On the homesteads and in the small villages pioneer men and women were linked together doing common tasks. Though duties were divided among members of a family or village, the performance of these duties was directly dependent on those performed by others, resulting in a way of life that was communal.

When the Western frontier closed, both the pioneer and the Indian cultures became extinct, and with them we lost the original mainstream of American life. Even the heritage that pioneer women passed down to their female descendants was forsaken as women were slowly cut off from their men and the public life of their communities. By being withdrawn from a shared and equal life in society, women finally lost the respect that they had held as full partners in the severe struggle for survival that characterized our early social history. The American women's gain in comforts and leisure must therefore be measured against their loss of status as well as by the dulling of their pioneer spirit. The gradual disappearance of women architects from American public life was one of the telling signs.

Footnotes

1. Ray Allen Billington, *America's Frontier Heritage* (New York, Holt, Rinehart and Winston, 1966) p. 215
2. Walter O'Meara, *Daughters of the Country* (New York, Harcourt, Brace and World, Inc., 1968), p. 54
3. Ibid, p. 52
4. Alice Marriott and Carol K. Rachlin, *American Epic: The Story of the American Indians* (New York, G. P. Putnam's Sons, 1961), p. 73
5. O'Meara, op. cit., p. 49
6. Reginald and Gladys Laubin, *The Indian Tipi, Its History, Construction and Use* (Norman, University of Oklahoma Press, 1957), p. VII
7. Ibid, p. 103
8. Ibid, p. 167
9. Mrs. Frances Trollope, *Domestic Manners of the Americans* (New York, Alfred A. Knopf, 1949), p. 89.
10. Marriott and Rachlin, op. cit., p. 182
11. William Current and Vincent Scully, *Pueblo Architecture of the Southwest* (Austin, University of Texas Press, 1971), p. 17
12. Fred Eggan, *Social Organization of the Western Pueblos* (Chicago, The University of Chicago Press, 1950), p. 33
13. Current and Scully, op. cit., p. 16
14. Stanley A. Stubbs, *Bird's-Eye View of the Pueblos* (Norman, University of Oklahoma Press, 1950), p. 19-20
15. Marriott and Rachlin, op. cit., p. 104
16. Jeannettee Henry Costo, notes on women in architecture sent to Doris Cole, April 9, 1973

2 EARLY AMERICAN PERIOD

The Domestic Domain

In the early decades of the nineteenth century, the typical pre-Civil War American was wary about the arts. Men were engrossed in politics and business ("The gentlemen spit, talk of elections and the price of produce, and spit again"[1]), while women occupied themselves with their homes and religion. Simplicity was considered highly virtuous by the Puritan ethic, which pervaded American life and brought with it a corresponding distrust of the arts, including architecture. Although fearing the association with luxury and corruption, people were not insensitive to the enjoyment of art and the need for the growing country to develop a cultural base. Painting, music, literature, and architecture were beginning to express the new society and, with increasing prosperity, the United States had, in time, to give them suitable recognition. On the one hand there was the urge to articulate in the arts the strong idealism of young America and on the other the need to justify cultural expressions according to the moral scruples of American Protestantism.

Mixed with the national pride of Americans at that time was the awareness that they were considered crude and uncultured in the eyes of the rest of the world. In 1831, after visiting the United States, Mrs. Trollope published her book, *Domestic Manners of the Americans.* It was widely read in America, and it caused an uproar, for she had criticized every place she visited, including such notable centers as Cincinnati, New Orleans, Washington, Boston, and New York. She found Americans to be a crude, uncultured people.

Not only did European visitors criticize Americans, but Americans themselves, though far more gently, suggested that this country improve its cultural habits. Like Emma Willard and Grace Greenwood, many Americans traveling to Europe at that time were impressed with the buildings, parks, and monuments. As Americans convinced themselves that art and architecture were beneficial to the public welfare, the demand for their expressions grew. The Reverend T. F. Dibdin and later the Reverend Henry Ward Beecher proclaimed art and architecture to be good for the soul. Like other leaders of their period, they supposed the citizenry could be inspired and the glories of God and Nation represented and taught through the arts. Monuments and buildings, songs and literature illustrating the political and moral virtues of the United States began to appear, including the Bunker Hill Monument in Boston, state capitol buildings, universities, Athenaeums, and the National Capitol in Washington, D.C. Neil Harris, in his book *The Artist in American Society*, describes this change of attitude in the United States. "Once frightened of the arts because they had so often been the tools of Church and State, enemies to freedom and equality, Americans now valued them precisely for their political uses."[2] Prosperous businessmen appeased their consciences by giving a little of their profits to civic projects and, though excluded from political life, women helped raise funds for undertakings like construction of the Bunker Hill Monument.

The clergy, certainly the most educated segment of the population, also were able to find their grounds for encouraging the arts. Despite their suspicions of the cathedrals and magnificent art works of the Roman Church, the American Protestant clergymen nevertheless could not help but see that the very things they loathed served the function of inspiring the faithful towards God as well as keeping them under clerical domination. Accordingly, the Protestant attitude towards the arts became one of absorption. In 1821 T. F. Dibdin translated from the French and adapted for English readers *A Treatise of the Education of Daughters*, in which he strongly criticized "knicknacks and gey gaws," but found virtue in the study of serious paintings. Henry Ward Beecher recommended collecting art and supporting fine architecture and, with other ministers, stressed the moral virtues which should be illustrated by, and form the guiding principles of, any work of art.

At the same time, their female contemporaries, whose domain was within the home, also looked for justifications of their interests in the arts and architecture. Or, perhaps more correctly, women used the political and religious arguments devised by politicians and clergy to justify what they had been doing from their first day on

As late as 1880 such towns as Hugoton, Kansas, were crude compared to the villages visited by American tourists in Europe.

the North American continent, which was to civilize the natural environment that they had found here. Now women could in good conscience arrange their homes, decorate their parlors, hang their curtains, paint their houses, fabricate their furniture, and collect art. A house comfortably and pleasing outfitted, though never in needless luxury, suited the moral objectives of our new and righteous democracy. Domestic architecture continued to progress along this philosophical line.

Though simplicity was certainly valued as an aesthetic principle in the United States, crudeness was not. Through trips to Europe, architectural handbooks on approved styles, treatises, and lectures, men and women set out to correct this evident condition. American towns and architecture were crude compared to European standards. Mrs. Trollope was appalled at the custom of throwing garbage in the streets of Cincinnati and letting bands of roving hogs come by to eat it up. She found the Eastern part of the United States a bit better, and noted that nearing Baltimore the houses looked adequate and comfortable and yards were neatly fenced. Of public buildings, the Catholic Cathedral in Baltimore suited her tastes; its interior was neat and almost elegant, though the art decorating the cathedral she judged terrible. Her son, the writer Anthony Trollope, traveled in the United States thirty years later and could only state that there were no public buildings which merited any special praise. Domestic architecture, East and West, was met with much greater enthusiasm by both Trollopes. In the East, Anthony Trollope found the Boston houses to be spacious and excellent; in the West, his mother had viewed some pretty dwellings while traveling down the Ohio River.

The architectural styles that gained popularity in America before the Civil War also reflected people's moral and political ideas. There were great debates as to which style of architecture properly reflected the principles of the young Republic. Men argued that the Egyptian obelisk style, used at the Washington Monument, was inappropriate, coming from an ancient culture without democratic principles. Though the obelisk and other historic forms had their supporters, the architecture of the Greeks was far more popular and was considered more appropriate for American ideals. Talbot Hamlin explains in *Greek Revival Architecture in America:* "The fact that decorative detail was based upon classic precedent, and especially upon Greek precedent, was due not merely to an increasing interest in archaeology, but more especially to the enthusiasm which the whole Western World, and particularly the new republic, showed for the struggles of Greece during her wars of independence." [3] In ancient Greece the Americans believed they had found the ideals of democracy and freedom. With this justification they used the Greek columns and capitals, decorations, and friezes they thought reflected the democratic principles of the ancient Greeks. And thus the so-called Greek Revival style of architecture became popular not only in the South but in the North and West of America. The admiration for Greek architecture was not found solely among men of public life. In 1839, Mrs. Louisa Tuthill advised that "a knowledge of the rise and progress of architecture, and its perfection under the classic Greeks, ought to be acquired by every well informed lady." [4]

In the first half of the nineteenth century there were very few professionally trained architects in America. And so it was "amateurs," people who had not received the professional training available in Europe and therefore did not follow its precepts in any literal manner, who built our country. Lacking a professional background, they were often original in their solutions to the architectural problems confronting them. This is not to say that people of this time, and women in particular, had no knowledge of architecture or lacked guidelines to follow when designing their homes and buildings. There were many books published and sold in America that gave suggested plans, aesthetic viewpoints, and methods of construction. *The Young Builder's General Instructor* (1829), *The Modern Builder's Guide* (1833), and *The Beauties of Modern Architecture* (1835), all written by Minard Lafever, were just a few of the hundreds of books produced in the United States. Americans bought these books written by carpenters, craftsmen, and enthusiasts, carrying this knowledge to all parts of the country.

Another category of books on architecture existed which rarely, if ever, is mentioned by architectural historians. And yet this category was probably the most influential in shaping domestic architecture in America. (Note, too, that American architecture of the nineteenth century was mainly composed of domestic buildings.) These publications, classified as "etiquette" books, were read mainly by women and for the most part were also written by women. *Letters to Young Ladies* (1833), *The Young Lady's Friend* (1837), *The Young*

Lady's Home (1847), *Woman in Her Various Relations* (1853), and *Manners* (1866): the list is endless. And this kind of book was read widely throughout the country, as popular in the East as in the West. Even the author of *Uncle Tom's Cabin*, Harriet Beecher Stowe, wrote books about architecture for women. She and her sister, Catherine Beecher, wrote the extremely detailed book, *The American Woman's Home* (1869), representing the culmination of Catherine's many years of teaching. These so-called "etiquette" books formed the platform from which women could speak to each other, could discuss frankly their views on domestic economy, and, most important, could share information on improving their practice of architecture. Such books guided the American woman in her attempt to create comfortable, attractive homes in a nation little interested in art.

During the first half of the nineteenth century, a woman's domain consisted of only two concerns — her home life and her religious life. It was noted by Mrs. Trollope that American women were occupied with the care of their homes and churches on a daily basis. The typical woman was strictly limited in her activities and interests: her life was a private one. Even her church work was not public in nature. She was tied to her family, often overburdened and overworked in her home because in this land of equality few wanted to be servants. In the slave states, also, the women of the family shared in the household work. Given a large household to manage without adequate hired help or today's technological aids in doing chores, for a woman of the 1800s to occupy herself outside of the home, except for charitable causes, was unthinkable. A respectable woman was dependent upon others, usually husband or family, for financial support, as was sadly noted by Mrs. Louisa Tuthill in 1839 when she explained that "so few are the ways in our country in which females can gain an honorable independence."[5] Society, and women as part of it, accepted the fact that a woman's duty was to manage her domestic realm as best she could and not to stray far from its physical and psychological borders.

When women were not occupied at home, they were most likely to be sewing for church missionaries, attending religious services, or entertaining visiting clergy and missionaries. The religious ministers were usually educated men and sympathetic to the women's desire for moral and cultural improvement. "With the priests of America, the women hold that degree of influential importance which, in the

H. M. Irwin.

Construction of Buildings.

Nº 94,116.   Patented Aug. 24, 1869.

Fig. 1.

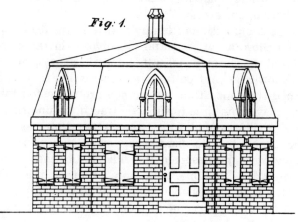

Fig. 2.

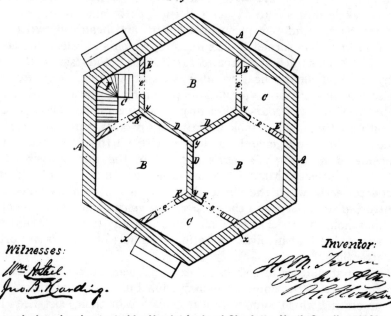

Witnesses: Inventor:

House designed and patented by Harriet Irwin of Charlotte, North Carolina, 1869.

countries of Europe, is allowed them throughout all orders and ranks of society," Mrs. Trollope observed in her American travels. Occupied with farming or business, husbands had little time for charitable works of the church. Accordingly, it was left to women to save their own souls and their husbands', too, if possible: "I never saw, or read, of any country where religion had so strong a hold upon the women, or a slighter hold upon the men."[6]

It was this combination of family and religious dedication which gained women the rank of "cultural preservers" in the eyes of men. Women not only performed difficult domestic chores, but strove to bring some knowledge and culture into men's lives. The American women warned their men that "as women are respected by the men of the age, so may, from time to time, be traced, by unerring measure, the degree of civilization to which that generation has attained."[7] They let men know that to disrespect women showed that America was still uncivilized and deserved the ridicule of other nations. The Englishwoman, Mrs. Trollope, was more blunt on the subject and stated that "the American people will not equal the nations of Europe in refinement till women become of more importance among them."[8]

The nineteenth-century woman, limited to her house and engulfed in domestic duties, turned her full energies to making her domain, no matter how limited, pleasant, efficient, and healthful. With this goal in mind she turned to architecture, which she called "domestic science." This included architectural style, good taste, economy, physical and mental health, supervision of workers, structure, site selection, heating and ventilation, plumbing, furniture design and fabrication, and, of course, efficient plan arrangements. Discussion at length on these topics took place among women through their etiquette books, and general familiarity with all this information was considered necessary to perform properly the duties assigned to women by society. Mrs. H. L. Signourney explained the female attitude correctly when she wrote that, "since the domestic sphere is entrusted to our sex, and the proper arrangement and government of a household are so closely connected with our enjoyments and virtues, nothing that involves the rational comfort of home is unworthy of attention."[9]

Nor should we forget that these American women were modest in their care of the domestic domain; few buildings have plaques on them stating which women were responsible for their existence. But then, few men were mentioned specifically, either. At that time the builders of this country were primarily anonymous. There was no mania, as there is today, for assigning a person's name to every structure erected. However, anonymity for women was more than compliance with the general cultural conditions of the age; it was a quality expected and encouraged in them. A woman was trained to be quiet in her manner, to say little in public, and to speak only when spoken to. This modesty of manner characterized her domestic life, for "honorable as is the performance of these daily duties, it is bad taste to say much about them." [10] Little was mentioned of women in the public records written by men, but in more private records — diaries and letters — women's interests and work appeared and were noted.

Knowing full well that the domestic domain was complicated and required knowledge, practicality, imagination, and ability to organize, women of the period compared the running of a house to the management of a government in its diversity and complexity. Clearly, they never felt that these were the duties of the stupid, since "the science of housekeeping affords exercise for the judgement and energy, ready recollection, and patient self possession, that are the characteristics of a superior mind." [11]

Women's admiration for the arts was great, and they were encouraged to read, study, and practice the arts. When Mrs. Louisa C. Tuthill complained that there were few ways for a woman to earn an honorable wage, she did include art as one method. Even without the necessity of earning an "honorable independence," a knowledge of art and architecture was considered essential by the ladies. In 1833 Mrs. Signourney insisted that "your course of reading should comprise the annals of Painting, Sculpture and Architecture. Perhaps, human genius has never displayed itself more gloriously than in these departments." [12] Greek architecture was preferred by many, and for the woman's "superior mind" it was strongly and frequently suggested that architecture, its orders and its principles of proportion, should be learned.

The women found that their knowledge of art could be applied in their daily lives and to their homes. With this practical orientation, they were not especially concerned with arguing about the merits of Greek or Egyptian styles. "The union and blending of colors, as taught in painting, enables one to know what colors best harmonize, and what are best in contrast." [13] Harmony of color was emphasized with specific suggestions of whitewashing the kitchen "to make

Drawing studio at the Philadelphia School of Design for Women founded in 1844 by Mrs. Sarah Worthington Peters to train women for employment in industrial arts.

it wholesome" and of painting the nursery a pale green since "it is easiest to the eye, and is a pleasing color." The selection of furniture did not escape the principles of taste when "in the ever-changing style of furniture there are always some rules that should govern taste and give supremacy."[14] Pictures were suggested to decorate the walls, although good engravings were found to be adequate. Advice and comments were endless and truly believed because "in the arrangement of a house, and the introduction of ornamental furniture, and articles of bijouterie, there can be no doubt of the inate superiority of women."[15] Not only did women assume themselves superior, but they considered themselves indispensable in bringing art and good taste to a home. As an example, one lady noted that "everyone must have remarked the difference in the furnishing of a bachelor's house, and one where a lady presides."[16]

Though art was their objective, economy was the necessity. Few families were wealthy, and women particularly had little command of money within the family. Balancing the domestic budget was a duty which necessarily involved "keeping accounts, the order and regulation of family expenses, the table, servants, furniture, visitors, etc., etc."[17] It was no easy task to provide the daily necessities and still have some money left for creating an attractive home. With this in mind, advice and helpful hints given in publications directed to women were pointed towards the need for economy. Again and again it was emphasized that good taste was not dependent upon great wealth, and that the value of material objects should be judged by their usefulness to human beings. The women explained that simplicity was actually good design, that too much furniture was uncomfortable, and that a love of luxury led to moral decline. In her book on architecture, Catherine Beecher stated that "in the description and arrangement, the leading aim is to show how time, labor, and expense are saved, not only in the building but in furniture and its arrangement." With this objective she and others described in precise detail how to fabricate houses, furniture, picture frames, and movable screens on a tight budget. With her sister, Harriet Beecher Stowe, Catherine Beecher even recommended that "the wood-work of the house . . . should be oiled chestnut, butternut, whitewood, and pine. This is cheaper, handsomer, and more easy to keep clean than painted wood." Inexpensive floor coverings, types of stoves, furnaces, and everything else pertinent to economy were scrutinized, not in vague terms, but with prices discussed to demonstrate the prin-

39

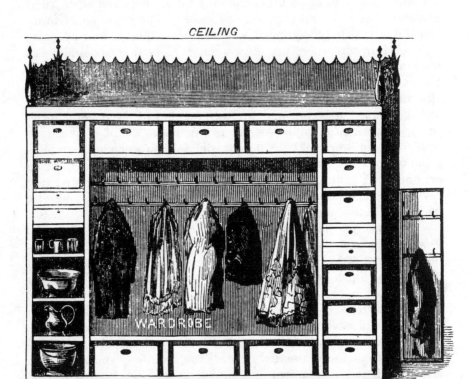

CEILING

WARDROBE

ROLLERS   ROLLERS

"The needless spaces usually devoted to kitchen, entries, halls, backstairs, pantries, store-rooms, and closets, by this method [the movable screen with storage units] would be used in adding to the size of the large room, so variously used by day and by night."
Beecher and Stowe, 1869.

ciple that good design could be had at reasonable cost. After describing the design and fabrication of her ingenious storage unit, Catherine Beecher explained that "the expense of the screen, where lumber averages $4 a hundred, and carpenter labor $3 a day, would be about $30, and the two couches about $6."[18] Throughout their many discussions, these women always emphasized that the comforts and beauties of art were available to the clever woman of modest means. They were not interested in the architectural problems of the wealthy; they addressed themselves to the majority of women and their difficulties in dealing with domestic architecture.

Aside from beauty and economy, the mental and physical health provided in their homes was uppermost in the minds of women. They felt that in their "hands rest the real destinies of the Republic, as molded by the early training and preserved amid the maturer influences of home."[19] Perhaps it was a naive view, but at that time the American women living on farms or in small towns considered themselves responsible for preserving the religious ideals underpinning the new nation.

In the early 1800s America was still a rural society. The domestic sphere not only encompassed all individuals within the household: it was the model of their world. With this preconception, women harnessed their architectural skills to enhance the health of the nation. Speaking for her contemporaries, Mrs. Hale advised that "in selecting or constructing a residence, health is, of course, the first consideration." Railroads were thought a blessing since men who worked in the cities could have their families living in the country. Suburban living was recommended for fresh air and exercise. The environmental concerns of women included site planning and selection. Mrs. Hale noted that "no one will — or at least should — fix his house on low and moist ground, when he can secure a high and dry foundation."[20] Along with the admonition to avoid excessive moisture went an advocacy of sunshine and pure air, with houses oriented to provide long periods of direct sunlight in rooms most used by the family. At the same time the Beechers were emphasizing that "the first and most indispensable requisite for health is pure air, both by day and night."[21] Through architecture, with its concern with site and building orientation, moisture and air control, women began to plan healthful homes for their families. They did not interpret architecture in narrow formal terms, but broadly enough to include these matters of health which were uppermost in their minds.

Neither did the technical complications of heating, ventilation, and plumbing escape the scrutiny of these self-trained women architects. To them these subjects were vital aspects of their domain. Certainly no home would have been beautiful, comfortable, economic, or healthful without proper heating, ventilation, and plumbing. Catherine Beecher felt that "every woman should be taught the scientific principles in regards to heat, and then their application to practical purposes." With this belief, she wrote an extremely long discourse on the scientific principles of conduction, convection, radiation, and reflection. Not only did she write on these matters, but taught them to her many pupils in Cincinnati, Ohio. Cooking stoves were discussed and along with them "one of the most serious evils in domestic life . . . chimneys that will not properly draw the smoke of a fire or stove." The numerous causes of and remedies for such chimneys were investigated thoroughly by Miss Beecher, while Mrs. Hale, among others, stressed the need for carefully planned ventilation in houses.

Humidity control also caught their attention since "there is no little wise economy in expense attained by keeping a proper supply

"After extensive inquiry and many personal experiments, [we have] found a cooking-stove constructed on true scientific principles . . ."
Beecher and Stowe, 1869.

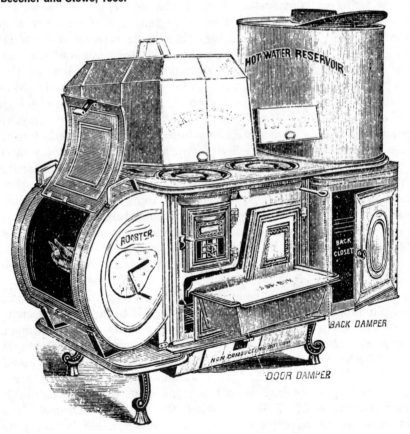

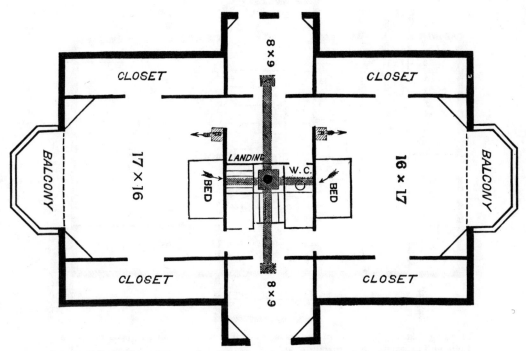

Second floor plan. "The main objection to attic rooms is their warmth in summer, owing to the heated roof. This is prevented by so enlarging the closets each side that their walls meet the ceiling under the garret floor . . ."
Beecher and Stowe, 1869.

of moisture in the air." With her detailed knowledge, Miss Beecher recommended the "ingenious instrument, called the hygrodeik, which indicates the exact amount of moisture in the air." The subject of plumbing was not neglected either, though certainly not all women could reach the degree of technical proficiency required to apply such suggestions as having "a reservoir in the garret, supplied by a forcing-pump in the cellar or at the sink" and seeing that "the water-closets . . . have the latest improvements for safe discharge, and there will be no trouble." [22]

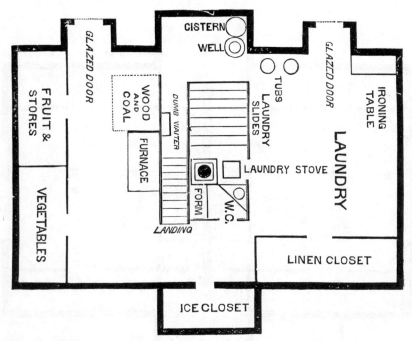

Basement plan. "The floor of the basement must be an inclined plane toward a drain, and be plastered with waterlime."
Beecher and Stowe, 1869.

Methods of construction as well as plan arrangements were considered of great importance by the women authors of these unofficial architectural books. They discussed at great length the types of wood to use, when brick was appropriate, what materials were best for floors and walls. It was suggested "never [to] use inferior materials in buildings because they are cheaper,"[23] explaining that such false economy only shortened the life of the house. The incline of the basement floor, the estimated construction budgets — practically every conceivable detail was covered by these women. The mortised joint was lauded and "a wash of gunishinglass [fish-glue]" was to be applied twice before white varnish. In floor plans for their houses,

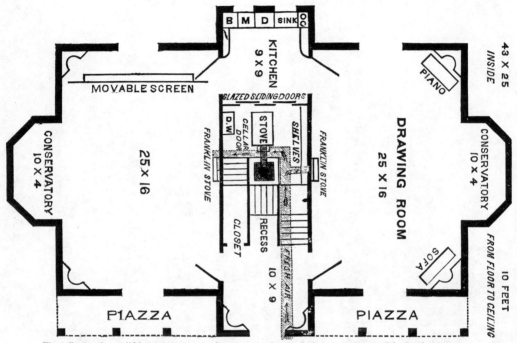

First floor plan. "Aim to secure a house so planned that it will provide in the best manner for health, industry, and economy, those cardinal requisites of domestic enjoyment and success."
Beecher and Stowe, 1869.

the women were no less thorough. To avoid constantly climbing stairs, Mrs. L. G. Abell recommended that the nursery, sitting-room, kitchen, and parlor be located on the same floor. Catherine Beecher and Harriet Beecher Stowe gave detailed plans with blow-ups of the kitchen, the arched recesses in the front hall, the sliding windows, and everything else that goes into the design of a house. Little escaped the critical eyes of these women: one of them, Grace Greenwood, sympathetically explained that the French kings went off to their villas and hunting lodges to escape the cold and stiff grandeur of the Louvre. These nineteenth-century American women — who in today's terminology might be labelled environmental design-

Residence by Harriet Beecher Stowe built with the first profits of *Uncle Tom's Cabin* in Hartford, Connecticut, 1863. This photo was taken many years later when the house had been sold to the Hartford Cycle Works and used as a storehouse.

ers — wanted to avoid the design mistakes they had seen at the Louvre and felt quite confident that they could.

These women not only had a broad knowledge of architecture, but they put it to specific use supervising construction. They did not always find their carpenters and workmen adequate, and they fell back on their own acquired training to guide the workmen. Usefulness was essential to them: Mrs. Hale even criticized the few so-called professional architects for their schemes on ventilation because "the plans which these propose are often so expensive and complicated as to deter many persons from adopting them." [24] She gave her own design for a good ventilation system, and so did Catherine Beecher to secure that "the plan is properly executed even with workmen so entirely ignorant on this important subject as are most house-builders, especially in the newer territories." Nor did the masons escape the wrath of these well informed women in regard to chimneys: "the artisans of the present day seem strangely ignorant of the true method of constructing them." [25] With their manuals in hand and a strong determination to construct pleasant, comfortable homes the American women of the nineteenth century let the "menfolk" saw, hammer, and nail, but they were always there suggesting and supervising.

These women grasped the essence of architecture. While the men spent much time discussing the fashionable and historically appropriate style of architecture for the growing nation, the women addressed themselves to more germane issues of architecture — the technological and social innovations that were occurring before their eyes. Mrs. Signourney wrote in 1833 that "the sphere of woman is eminently practical." [26] In fact, the sphere of architecture is still, as it was then, eminently practical. Style has never been the essence of architecture. For the women who planned and built nineteenth-century America, architecture did not mean the lavish monument or the estate of the wealthy, but economical, soundly constructed, well ventilated buildings conducive to the physical and mental well-being of the ordinary family. All of the practical and aesthetic considerations were to lead to the greater joy, comfort and moral improvement of the nation's inhabitants: this was the aim of these women architects.

One of the strongest supporters of women in architecture was Harriet Beecher Stowe, who actually designed her own house in

Hartford, Connecticut, in 1863. Mrs. Stowe wrote that "one of the greatest reforms that could be, in these reforming days . . . would be to have women architects. The mischief with houses built to rent is that they are all mere male contrivances." She found that "architecture and landscape gardening are arts every way suited to the genius of woman, and there are enough who have the requisite mechanical skill and mathematical education." The visionary Mrs. Stowe hoped that "when women plan dwelling-houses, the vast body of tenements to be let in our cities will wear a more domestic and comfortable air, and will be built more with reference to the real wants of their inmates."[27] Calvert Vaux also wrote affirmatively on this subject. In his book *Villas and Cottages*, published in 1864, he put forth a rather gracious argument in behalf of his female contemporaries.

There can be no doubt that the study of domestic architecture is well suited to a feminine taste, and it has, moreover, so many different ramifications, that it affords frequent opportunities for turning good abilities to profitable account; for if we even allow the objections that might be raised by some against the actual practice of architecture by women, such as the necessity for their climbing ladders, mingling with the mechanics and laborers during the progress of the works . . . we must, nevertheless see at once that there is nothing in the world, except want of inclination or opportunity, to prevent many of them from being thoroughly expert in architectural drawings, or from designing excellent furniture . . .

I do not, it will be perceived, include in the difficulties to be overcome want of natural ability, for this certainly does not exist . . .[28]

Perhaps the forecasts of Mrs. Stowe and Mr. Vaux were too optimistic. Although they realized that there were no inherent limitations to women's capabilities in architecture, they underestimated the social structures that continued to keep women within the confines of their private domestic domains.

In fact, as the country industrialized, women's isolation from society worsened. More people lived in cities, and cities changed the economic, social, and political balances of rural America. A direct consequence was that an ever-increasing proportion of men left their homesteads for outside work. The homestead that once had comprised both the domestic and economic base of family life was fractured. Men and women were now clearly separated in their work and scope of responsibilities.

Footnotes

1. Mrs. Frances Trollope, *Domestic Manners of the Americans* (New York, Alfred A. Knopf, 1949, first published in London 1831), p. 58
2. Neil Harris, *The Artist In American Society, The Formative Years 1790-1860* (New York, George Braziller, Inc., 1966), p. 160
3. Talbot Hamlin, *Greek Revival Architecture in America* (New York, Dover Publications, Inc., 1964), p. xvi
4. Mrs. Louisa C. Tuthill, *The Young Lady's Home* (Boston, William J. Reynolds and Company, 1847), p. 71
5. Ibid, p. 71
6. Trollope, op. cit., p. 75
7. A Lady, *The Lady's Companion or Sketches of Life, Manners & Morals, at the present day* (Philadelphia, H. C. Peck & Theo. Bliss, 1852), p. 8
8. Trollope, op. cit., p. 422.
9. Mrs. L. H. Sigourney, *Letters To Young Ladies* (Hartford, William Watson, 1835) first edition 1833, p. 27
10. A Lady, *The Young Lady's Friend* (Boston, American Stationers' Company, John B. Russell, 1837), p. 41
11. Ibid, p. 27
12. Sigourney, op. cit., p. 81
13. Mrs. L. G. Abell, *Woman In Her Various Relations* (New York, R. T. Young, 1853), p. 78
14. Ibid, p. 90, 77
15. A Lady, *The Lady's Companion,* op. cit., p. 37
16. Ibid, p. 37
17. Tuthill, op. cit., p. 148
18. The three quotations preceding this footnote in the text are from Catherine E. Beecher and Harriet Beecher Stowe, *The American Woman's Home* (New York, J. B. Ford and Company, 1869), p. 25, 41, 32
19. Ibid, Dedication
20. The two quotations preceding this footnote in the text are from Mrs. Hale, *Manners* (Boston, J. E. Tilton, 1868), p. 65, 66
21. Beecher and Stowe, op. cit., p. 43
22. This footnote applies to the quotations in the two preceding paragraphs.
    Ibid, p. 66, 76, 67, 81, 36, 38
23. Hale, op. cit., p. 71
24. Ibid, p. 67
25. Beecher and Stowe, op. cit., p. 76, 64

26. Sigourney, op. cit. p. 36
27. The three quotations in the preceding paragraph come from Harriet Beecher Stowe, *Household Papers and Stories* (Boston, Houghton Mifflin & Co., 1896), first copyright in 1864 by H. B. Stowe, p. 188, 257
28. Calvert Vaux, *Villas and Cottages* (Franklin Square, New York, Harper & Brothers, 1857), p. 236-237

The United States Sanitary Commission at Fredericksburg, 1864.

3 SOCIAL TRANSITIONS
From Domestic to Civic Domains

Though occupied with their families and domestic duties, women of the late 1800s were also concerned with religious and intellectual pursuits. Mrs. Hale explained the woman's viewpoint when she wrote that "man is the worker or provider, the protector and law-giver; woman is the preserver, the teacher or inspirer, and the exemplar."[1] The female authors of the "etiquette" books divided domestic duties from intellectual pursuits. Management of a household was not considered an intellectual activity: one lady went so far as to advise that "better would it have been for her never to have had a flower in the house, than . . . to neglect the more important duties of mental culture."[2] Women like Catherine Beecher were dedicated to transforming domestic duties into the profession of domestic science, and with this in mind they investigated architectural and scientific knowledge necessary for running a household. But others — women like Harriet Beecher Stowe, Margaret Fuller, Clara Barton, and Charlotte Forten Grimké — went beyond their own homes, pursuing strong religious, intellectual, and political interests.

In the beginning of the nineteenth century it was customary for women to confine their interest to, and in turn be cared for by, their families. As the century progressed, this situation changed slowly but irrevocably. In 1878 Mrs. H. O. Ward explained that "owing to the changes in social and industrial life which have crowded many women from the privacy of their homes into the arena of public life, they must select their branch of labor and train for it."[3] The Civil War, industrialization, urbanization, fluctuating class structure: many factors changed the realities of the American woman's life.

Married and unmarried women began to face the fact that they could not rely upon their husbands and families for adequate financial support. Financial need, indeed, had been one of the factors in the careers of such women as Harriet Beecher Stowe and Louisa May Alcott. Although women and men accepted the tenet that "man is the worker or provider," the reality was often far different. Women were often unmarried, widowed, deserted, or married to financially insolvent spouses. Young European women immigrated to America without their families in the hope of finding work. Even as early as 1833 Mrs. Sigourney saw this problem clearly and strongly believed "it desirable that young ladies should make themselves the mistresses of some attainment, either in art or science, by which they might secure a subsistance, should they be reduced to poverty."[4]

Society viewed women as the "cultural preservers," and perhaps this view had some influence on their choice of occupation. For example, women entered the fields of teaching, social service, and nursing; they worked with orphans and benevolent societies. Since they had, from the period of the earliest settlers, been active in sewing circles, church societies, and the dispensing of homely medicines, to enter such fields was not an unnatural transition. Florence Nightingale became a heroine for her nursing work in the Crimean War, and her example elevated nursing from housework to a profession. Women had been the teachers for their children at home and then, as education became institutionalized, in the schools. The transformation of what were once considered womenly interests into occupations was increasingly acceptable to society, especially if a woman was in financial need, in line with the duty ascribed to the American woman by society and herself as the "cultural preserver."

Catherine Beecher and Harriet Beecher Stowe affirmed the domestic function of woman, in whose "hands rest the real destinies of the Republic, as moulded by the early training and preserved amid the matured influences of home."[5] However, to sustain this belief as the century progressed was difficult, if not impossible. The havoc wrought by the Civil War alone was enough to make women realize that the domestic domain was not isolated from exterior influences. A woman could organize her home, beautify her house, and instruct her family — but none of these accomplishments could save her men and children from the sorrows of war. With these experiences in mind, women from the Northern states created the United States Sanitary Commission just two months after the defeat at Fort Sumter.

The aim of the Sanitary Commission was to inspect and regulate the conditions of the army camps and hospitals during the Civil War.

Present at the Western front along the Mississippi River and at the Battle of Shiloh, the Commission followed the army to Bull Run and Gettysburg and tried to alleviate the sordid conditions of military camps near Washington. Located near mosquito-infested, stagnant swamps, the camp sites were covered with debris and garbage. Mud was knee deep when it rained, a cloud of suffocating dust covered the area when it was dry, rivers and streams were soon polluted, and the dying were quartered in stifling tents. The soldiers were responsible for cooking their own food, a skill which few had acquired at home, but even the best cook would have been hard put to turn the regulation salt pork, hardtack, beans, and coffee into a nourishing meal. Cooked in old grease, the smells spread for miles around the camp, mingling with the odors of garbage, sweat, urine, and disease.

The history of the United States Sanitary Commission shows how much it was the women's undertaking. In 1861 Dr. Elizabeth Blackwell, the first woman doctor in the country, met with others to discuss the idea. Soon after, a large and enthusiastic meeting was held to organize and choose delegates to go to Washington for authorization. The official delegates sent to Washington were all men, but even they met with little encouragement from Lincoln, the Surgeon General, or the Secretary of War. The women forced them to persist, and finally permission was granted to work among the volunteer troops. The Sanitary Commission was an independent organization with no financial aid from the government. It was the women who understood the need, raised the money, and did the work.

Women did not just stay at home wrapping bandages — they went to the front line to clean, cook, nurse, inspect and supervise, often staying for months and even years. The women of the Sanitary Commission sent experts to help the regimental surgeons choose sites, enforce healthful sanitary conditions within the camps, and inspect the cooking. Many of these experts were women like Florence Nightingale, Dorothea Dix (Superintendent of Army Nurses), Mrs. Mary Ann Bicherdyke, and Mrs. William Preston Griffin. Their objective was to bring some humane and domestic comfort to the men away from their homes. The Sanitary Commission's investigation after the Battle of Bull Run found that clean camps with good discipline produced courageous soldiers. The women had created upright citizens from their domestic domains, and now they were going to try to create brave soldiers from their new turf, the military camp.

A part of their work involved nursing the wounded. To reach the wounded of the battlefield was always a problem, and this the women solved with portable architecture. They suggested the architectural solution of hospital boats, and the Hospital Transport Service was begun, transforming steamers into efficient hospitals. Such hospital boats as "City of Memphis" and "Emerald" were often there before the battle even began, waiting for the inevitable horde of wounded and dying men. These floating portable hospitals worked well, bringing supplies and staff down the rivers and transporting the wounded to more permanent hospitals away from the battleline. There was nothing abstract here, nothing remote about their experience: "All these steamers had busy women on board . . . They were perhaps the most outstanding group of women front-line workers the war produced."[6]

The victory of the North in the Civil War brought greater freedom to the Negro slaves and also, in some respects, to white women. Little did the women of the Sanitary Commission, the nurses, and other volunteers realize that they were in fact fighting for their own freedom. During the Civil War the traditional restrictions and conventions governing women's activities were ignored, not as a matter of choice, but to meet the demands of war. Women had functioned well in their war organizations: they had gained confidence in their abilities in that larger domain which many of them had craved. Many women never went back to their homes: these were the transitional women, wishing desperately to be occupied beyond the domestic, seeing clearly the needs of their nation, constantly being hampered by government and established society, dragging behind them the more conservative reluctant ladies of the day.

The state of these active women was best described by Kate Gannett Wells in her article of 1885, "Transitional Woman." "The face of to-day," she declared, "is stamped with restlessness, wandering purpose, and self-consciousness." Many women were no longer satisfied with the domestic, which seemed increasingly meaningless in its sphere of influence and annoying in its demands. Women became more vocal in their dislike of housework, and the home was "no longer the focus of *all* their endeavors." Clara Barton, Harriet Beecher Stowe, Florence Nightingale, Margaret Fuller, Edith Wharton, Dr. Elizabeth Blackwell, Louisa May Alcott, Frances Willard, Mary Safford — women like these lived active lives in which they were free to work and think. Other women saw their examples and wished to follow their lead. Kate Wells advised the "transitional woman" to "do something, be of worth in yourself, form opinions." This attitude was "the imperative mood in which the times address modern woman."[7]

Opportunities arose for women seeking to expand their domestic domain in teaching and social service. In the industrialized regions of post-Civil-War America life changed and cities grew. Here the middle- or upper-class woman found a chance to apply her knowledge and architectural skills to the plight of the disadvantaged immigrants and workers found within the growing cities. Having directed the servants and hired-help within her home, she was unfortunately all too likely to approach them like Mrs. Sigourney, who condescendingly commented that "among the pleasant employments which seem peculiarly congenial to the feelings of our sex, the culture of lowers stands conspicuous."[8] In the past the American woman, typically "the exemplar," had used her cultural and architectural knowledge to influence the morals of her independent domestic domain. Now that domain was no longer isolated and secure in its influence upon its members. It was located within a city, and the city encroached upon its privacy. Through social services a woman could continue using her practical skills, but on a larger scale, and, hopefully, influence more than just her own family and servants. In this sense her domain encompassed the city, and her family became the entire citizenry.

In the last part of the nineteenth century and in the early twentieth century women like Jane Addams emerged to establish settlement houses among destitute industrial workers and immigrants. Miss Addams and her colleagues opened Hull House in Chicago on September 14, 1889. The mansion they occupied had been built in a once-rural part of Chicago predicted by speculators to have a prosperous future, but the city's direction of growth changed, leaving the Hull Mansion surrounded by dismal tenements. By any standards the mansion was spectacular, with finely worked stone walls, huge spaces, and numerous rooms. As a young girl, Miss Addams had dreamed of owning such a house, not for her own personal use but for her friends — and to her, the poor were her friends. This grandest of homes was now open to the workers for social and political meetings, for a children's nursery, for classes in homemaking, art, or anything her friends might choose.

Jane Addams with art student.

The realities of life in this part of Chicago were hard and raw. The Hull House staff confronted problems far more terrible than any of them had experienced in their own lives. Men, women, and children lived and worked in the sweat shops located in old wooden tenements without water or adequate ventilation, plumbing, heat, or light. Disease was everywhere in the decaying buildings. If Jane Addams and her staff were to accomplish anything, they must find specific solutions to these conditions.

Jane Addams attacked these problems on every front. She was called a social reformer, not an architect, but she knew that architecture was concerned with where and how people lived. She realized that architecture for these people could mean part of the solution to the daily despair and miseries derived from an inadequate physical environment. Even to begin work on these problems was a tremendous task. She sought the support of the politically powerful in Illinois, and these people helped her by passing child-labor laws, controlling sweat shops, clearing garbage, building playgrounds, and working on a hundred other projects.

One of the staff members of Hull House was a young woman interested in the arts named Ellen Starr. She taught at the settlement house for many years, attempting to bring some pleasure into the drab, ugly, crowded households surrounding Hull House. As a result of her work and influence the first addition to Hull House in 1891 was the Butler Picture Gallery. Exhibits were put on for the people in the neighborhood. Here was a breathing place, an oasis for society's neglected to escape for a while the bleakness of their dwellings.[9]

Not only in the cities but in the rural South among the freed, though neglected, blacks, women worked and taught. Some of these women were white, middle-class activists, but many were former slaves, who met the tremendous challenge of first educating themselves and then returning home to help better the lives of their own black people. Though it was often illegal to educate slaves, a few blacks learned to read and write from sympathetic white friends, mistresses, or at clandestine schools run by such black women as Mary Peake of Hampton, Virginia. Susie King Taylor, who later nursed and taught black Civil War soldiers, recalled that her white playmate, Katie O'Connor, "told me, if I would promise not to tell her father, she would give me some lessons. On my promise not to do so, and gaining her mother's consent, she gave me lessons about four months every evening."[10]

The black women's plight was far more severe than their white counterparts. Before the Civil War, the houses they tended belonged to their masters; their own homes were little more than shacks. What part black women had in Southern architecture is unrecorded and unknown, but they labored from morning to night in the fields and at the mansions. After picking cotton all day, then doing the regular chores, "finally, at a late hour, they reach the quarters, sleepy and overcome with the long day's toil. Then a fire must be kindled in the cabin, the corn ground in the small hand-mill, and supper, and dinner for the next day in the field, prepared."[11]

One example among many black women was Mary McLeod Bethune, who founded Bethune Cookman College in 1904. First educated by "a young woman, a colored missionary sent by the Northern Presbyterian Church," she continued her studies at Scotia Seminary in Concord, North Carolina, aided financially by a white dressmaker. Mrs. Bethune opened her own school in Florida without money but with "faith in a living God, faith in myself, and a desire to serve."[12] With architectural ingenuity, Mary Bethune created a schoolhouse for her first students.

We burned logs and used the charred splinters as pencils and mashed elderberries for ink. I begged strangers for a broom, a lamp, a bit of cretonne to put around the packing case which served as my desk. I haunted the city dump and the trash piles behind hotels, retrieving discarded linen and kitchenware, cracked dishes, broken chairs, pieces of old lumber. Everything was scoured and mended. This was part of the training to salvage, to reconstruct, to make bricks without straw . . . I had to provide sleeping accommodations. I took corn sacks for mattresses. Then I picked Spanish moss from trees, dried and cured it, and used it as a substitute for mattress hair.[13]

Women like Jane Addams were greatly admired by the nation as a whole, while active black women were known to their own race. Through these examples, other women were encouraged to occupy themselves with teaching and the social services. Dominated by women and considered women's work, these fields were unpopular with white men and rarely open to black men. The social services, just like the women's Civil-War efforts, developed as an extension and enlargement of women's domestic domain. The private domestic domain had included the solution of a number of basic practical architectural problems. Though society did not call this architecture, it was, in fact, just that. As woman's domestic domain expanded from her house (or her master's house) to the community at large, she continued to use her skill in architecture, trying to create a suitable physical environment for their communities.

The traditional domestic domain had separated women from men: these new activities in the social services did the same. Though women had expanded their domain, it was still a feminine domain. Women had not joined men; they had created new fields of activity for themselves. As blacks and the diversified ethnic groups integrated into conventional middle-class American society, they were subjected to, and often willingly adopted, the sexual divisions and domain definitions. Economically and politically, men and women still were not equal according to the laws of this nation. To fulfill their goal of equality and their desire to work together, thousands of men and women left conventional society to join or found the numerous communes in the United States.

In the 1800s communes sprang up across the country, experimenting with a variety of utopian systems aimed at providing a better life on earth and a surer path to heaven. There were hundreds of these communities established by the Moravians, Shakers, Rappites, True Inspirationists of Amana, Perfectionists of Oneida, Owenites, Fourierists, Hutterites, Society of Brothers, Separatists, and others. The life of these communes ranged from two years to over two hundred, with some still existing today. Often their economies were envied by conventional businessmen and were surprisingly productive. Following various philosophies, some communes were ruled by committees, others by one strong leader, but most shared the principles of equality for all people regardless of race or sex, rejection of private property, disbelief in the traditional norms of official churches and society, and refusal to involve themselves in violence, particularly war. New architectural forms often resulted from these nonconforming ideas and lifestyles.

Charles Nordhoff, an American journalist, was one of many visitors to the communes who found their methods both curious and intriguing. In 1875 he published his book *The Communistic Societies of the United States*, which described his visits to over fifteen different communes. After extensive research, he attributed much of

Shaker Village.

their success to the equal inclusion of women in all facets of communal life.

In a commune, which is only a large family, I think it a great point gained for success to give the women equal rights in every respect with men. They should take part in the business discussions, and their consent should be as essential as that of the men in all the affairs of the society. This gives them, I have noticed, contentment of mind, as well as enlarged views and pleasure in self-denial. Moreover, women have a conservative spirit, which is of great value in a communistic society as in a family; and their influence is always toward a higher life.[14]

The Perfectionists, led by John Humphrey Noyes, established their society at Oneida, New York, in 1848. Transformed into the Oneida Company, Limited, in 1880, it is still going strong today. Their communal organization was one of the most controversial because of the practice of complex marriages. Though outsiders interpreted this as free love, it was hardly that. The central ruling committee had sole power to approve and match couples, with the chosen retaining the right to reject his or her selected mate. Birth control was one of the founding religious principles of this society and was used to free both women and the community from unwanted children. At Oneida women were as free as men, and life was organized to protect that freedom. Though women still cooked the food, breakfast was the only hot meal served, the rest being self service. After the age of fifteen months, children lived in the Children's House and were raised by members expert in child care. The women bobbed their hair and invented a new costume consisting of a calf-length skirt with slim trousers beneath. Men and women shared in farming, manufacturing, and manual labor, including the construction of the Mansion House and other communal buildings. Aside from their common work, women and men shared equally in the intellectual life of the commune; together they discussed and decided the direction and goals of their labor.[15]

Their philosophical attitudes were reflected in their architecture; individual family houses were unnecessary when there were no individual families. The members lived together in the large Mansion House, using a communal kitchen, dining room, reading room, and meeting area. One wing was devoted to the children and their guardians, while another provided sleeping quarters for adults.

Together the men and women labored, and together they determined the physical form of their environment.

Not only at Oneida, but at the other communes women and men were building new lives and new architecture. When Charles Nordhoff visited Amana, Iowa, in 1875, he found a woman heading the government, though only the male members of the society elected the ruling body. Here conventional marriage was practiced and each family had its own house, but to facilitate the communal life a common cook-house and prayer house were used by all. They were a people professing the simple life, permitting no steeples on the churches and no paint on the houses. They produced a striking, plain, straightforward architecture reflecting the austerity of their religious beliefs.

One of the most successful and enduring of these societies were the Shakers. By 1860 the Shakers had 6,000 members located in eighteen villages from Maine through Ohio. Their lives were strictly ordered according to their religious and social beliefs, among which were the duality of God (composed of male and female elements), celibacy, common ownership of property, public confession of sin, pacifism, spiritual expression through song and dance, and the equality of men and women. A woman, Ann Lee, brought the first Shakers to America in 1774, and women continued to share equally with men in all aspects of Shaker life. The entire government of the Shakers was based upon the male and female duality of God. At the head was the Central Ministry, consisting of two women and two men; next followed the Ministry of each village, the Elders and Elderesses, the Deacons and Deaconesses for each extented family. Though celibacy was strictly enforced, each family consisted of thirty to ninety men and women carefully separated sexually but always joined spiritually. Women were equal to men, but that did not mean each person was equal to the next. The Shakers did not elect their officials; in principle the leaders emerged naturally through divine inspiration, but, in fact, the Central Ministry chose the leaders for the various communities and to fill their own places. The common members followed their leaders, who supposedly had more direct communication with God and the spirit of Mother Ann.

The Millenium Laws recorded in 1821 by Father Joseph Meacham and Mother Lucy Wright and revised in 1845 were the most important set of rules guiding Shaker life. Here the orders for practically every activity of the Society and its members were codi-

Group of Shaker women and men.

fied, including how to walk, talk, pray, sleep, dress, eat, drink, work, etc., and when to do each of these activities. Though seemingly restrictive and rigid, it was not the aim of the Ministry to be inflexible, since they clearly stated that the Millenium Laws were guidelines and should always be open to revision and interpretation by the Elders.

Not only did the Millenium Laws deal with personal conduct and work habits, it formulated a strong philosophy to be followed in all of the Shaker buildings, furniture, decoration, and objects. Simplicity, usefulness, and modesty were principles that resulted not in drabness but in remarkable ingenuity. They invented the flat broom, the circular saw, the metal pen, a tongue-and-groove machine, a revolving oven, and an improved wood-burning stove. They were constantly bettering their systems of lighting, ventilation, heating, refrigeration, and washing. They believed that hand labor was good for the soul and the economy, but members rarely specialized in one occupation, having found that variety was much pleasanter for the worker. Each person was encouraged, therefore, to develop several skills, the individual deciding through conscience which work he or she wished to do. Even though individual ingenuity and skills were fostered, anonymity was required by the Millenium Laws. Section XII stated that "no one should write or print his name on any article of manufacture, that others may hereafter know the work of his hands."

The study of architecture was specifically included in the general studies for children, and greatly concerned Father Meacham and Mother Lucy Wright in several sections of the Millenium Laws. In Section IX they ordered that "odd or fanciful styles of architecture may not be used among Believers, neither should any deviate widely from the common style of building among Believers, without the union of the Ministry." They required that the Meeting House be painted white outside with a light blue shade on the interior; floors in the dwelling houses were to be stained a reddish yellow; barns and back buildings, if painted at all, were to receive a darker hue than buildings on the street; beadings, mouldings, and cornices were forbidden; varnish was only for moveable furniture; white, or a modest color, was recommended for curtains in the retiring rooms. The Laws covered a variety of architectural problems giving very specific rules to create an orderly, harmonious environment within each building and throughout the entire village.

Interior of Shaker kitchen.

The social structure, of course, influenced the architecture. Each extended family had its own building with separate doors and staircases for the men and women, sleeping rooms to accommodate two to six people, a common kitchen, dining room, and meeting room. Within the village were the large Meeting House, various shops for the sisters and brethren, the Trustees House, the communal wash house, the barns and out buildings. The families were self-sufficient, and they constructed the buildings necessary for carrying out their work.[16]

Today there are Shaker communities in Maine and New Hampshire, though only fourteen women are left. There are active Historical Societies in New England and Kentucky that preserve Shaker architecture, furniture, writings, and music. In Concord, Massachusetts, furniture of Shaker design is still being manufactured, while collectors of Americana covet Shaker originals.

While the women of the 1800s formed the United States Sanitary Commission and created the social services, the women who left conventional society found far greater opportunities for self development within the communes. Unfortunately these utopian communes had little effect upon established society. The majority of citizenry in nineteenth century America found it impossible to accept many of the revolutionary principles, and the alternative of stepping outside of society was not generally upheld as a goal.

Though Harriet Beecher Stowe and many others believed that architecture was an ideal profession for women, practically no women entered that field. Women were nurses, teachers, and social workers, but not professional architects. Although they made use of their architectural skills under the extraordinary conditions brought about by the Civil War and in the new field of social services, they did not enter the profession of architecture directly. The American woman's domain was in transition, and what would seem to be a most logical practice — architecture — was considered totally illogical within traditional cultural, social, educational, and economical contexts.

Only such people as Catherine Beecher felt that domestic science should be a profession, and even she always linked it with a woman's own home. Architecture, to the typical nineteenth century American woman, was one, and only one, of her many tools to provide for the physical and moral well being of her family and, later, the community at large. Again and again it was emphasized that it was a woman's

Shaker village at Canterbury, New Hampshire.

duty and aim "to uphold the religious ideas of the world, and to propagate them."[17] This justified her architectural interest, even though there were those like Mrs. Stowe, E. C. Gardner, and Calvert Vaux who recognized that women's architectural ability had an intrinsic value to the profession, apart from any moral or religious considerations. These few saw that the so-called domestic skills were the skills of an architect. While women had tried to elevate the value of domestic science, in the minds of women and society in general the division persisted, with a lower status given to the management of a household than to male professional and intellectual pursuits. The direct connection between the solutions of practical architectural problems related to daily life and what were presumed to be the concerns of the profession of architecture was appreciated by very few. It was to be many years before women officially entered the architectural profession and unwittingly brought with them those skills and attitudes which had become part of their social conditioning. Both the interested public and the architectural profession gave their major attention to a building's appearance, and in their choice of style followed the Beaux Arts tradition of Europe. At this time architectural students in the United States applied the Classical, Gothic, and Renaissance orders. Architects involved themselves in the requirements of prisons, hospitals, state capitols, and monuments, but uppermost in their minds was the idea of architecture as an art, with all of its manifestations of style. The emphasis was on the monumental, as exemplified by the Louvre. Grace Greenwood, however, found the Louvre simply uncomfortable and unpleasant, and clearly stated the woman's attitude towards the monumental when she wrote that "to my mind, the grandest palaces of Genoa are the charitable institutions . . . really the homes for the homeless."[18] Women, of course, learned the architectural styles, but academic discussions on style were simply alien to their concerns for an efficient home and moral health.

Though the professional architect did have to involve himself in technical and practical problems related to the buildings he designed, he thought of himself as an artist, an artist who created buildings rather than paintings or statues. Along with artisans and artists associated with him he considered utilitarian interests vulgar and intruding on the prerogatives of pure design. Women, on the other hand, whether rich or poor, had to work with daily and often annoying environmental conditions in trying to create a comfortable home

The Browne and Nichols School in Cambridge, Massachusetts, by Minerva Parker Nichols, 1897.

Minerva Parker was one of the few women who practiced architecture professionally in the 1800s. Though she studied at the Philadelphia Normal Art School and the Franklin Institute, her training began in January 1882 when she obtained a job as draftswoman with the Philadelphia architect Frederick G. Thorn, Jr. When Thorn retired in 1888, Miss Parker took over the work and successfully conducted her architectural practice for the next seven years. During those years she designed many private homes, two factories, women's clubs; and entered the competition for the Women's Building at the Columbian Exposition in Chicago. Unfortunately, in 1896 she left Philadelphia with her husband, Mr. Nichols, and thereafter confined her architectural practice to occasional projects for friends and relatives.

for their families and a community responsive to their needs. Harriet Beecher Stowe recognized that it was just this female attitude which was needed in the profession of architecture. She and her contemporaries knew that their intimate involvement with efficient planning, economy and utility in a building's heating, ventilation, plumbing, and structure was exactly what was often lacking in both domestic and civil architecture.

House Wins Prize

Mrs. Bertha Yerez Whitman, architect, 2656 Lincolnwood drive, won a special award in the Better Homes contest conducted by the Builders' exposition, 228 North LaSalle street, Chicago. The prize winning plans and photographs were those of the home of B. G. Lawrence, 2710 Payne street, and were submitted to the contest committee last January.

The plan of the first floor is unique, with the rooms large, well placed and conveniently arranged. The front door opens on a vestibule from which a second door leads into a hall which bisects the first floor of the house and opens on a large screened porch in the rear. A door to the right as one enters the hall leads into the living room which occupies that entire half of the lower floor and measures 12 ft., 6 in. by 24 ft., 4 in. There is a large brick fireplace on the outside wall with a window on either side and another window in the front wall. French doors in the rear open on the screened porch.

To the left after entering the hall are French doors which open into the dining room, and back of the dining room is the kitchen and breakfast nook. The stairways to the second floor and to the basement are both in the main hall, the one to the basement is enclosed and entered from a door at the rear while the one leading to the second floor is of the open balustrade design. Near the foot of the stairway is a large cloak closet for the use of visitors and guests.

There are four bedrooms and a bath on the second floor. Each bedroom has a closet opening from it, and in the rear bedroom over the livingroom there is a set of French doors opening upon the roof of the rear porch which is surrounded by a low balustrade giving it a balcony effect.

The house is a distinctly modern type built of red brick and having a portico front entrance, a large rear porch, and an outside entrance for the service stairway to the basement.

Bertha Yerex Whitman did receive her Bachelor of Science degree in Architecture from the University of Michigan in 1920. She has maintained a small private practice for fifty years consisting of private houses, churches, and apartments; in 1932 she designed the Woman's booth at the Chicago World's Fair; for eighteen years she handled all phases of engineering and supervision for offices of the Division of Unemployment Compensation. In 1973, at the age of eighty-one, Ms. Whitman is still busy practicing architecture, traveling around the world, and publishing her book *A Tyro Takes A Trip.*

Another obstacle blocking women from entering the architectural profession was society's prevalent attitude toward business. Business was, and for that matter still is, a male occupation and certainly, by nineteenth century mores, not the place for a lady; teaching, nursing, and social service were not considered business activities and were therefore acceptable areas of work for cultured women. Architecture, in fact, was just as much a business as an art. An architect needed clients, and to get clients meant hustling, selling, mixing with politicians to fight and even to bribe for jobs. It was necessary to find clients with money, and these clients came from the industrial, political, and financial arenas where women had little influence. Moreover, women did not vote or hold public office and, according to law, were not even able to sign contracts. With all these factors, it would have been very difficult for a woman of that time to develop an architectural practice.

Of course, women entered the business world, but as low-level employees — factory workers in New England mills and in the sweat shops of America's burgeoning industries. These women had neither the education, leisure time, nor money to pursue a training in architecture. This elimination of middle- and upper-class women from business and professional occupations had serious consequences. In effect, it relegated the American woman to the home and kept her from assuming an equal place in society. This was as true in architecture as in any other area.

Not only did conditions in society eliminate women from active architectural careers, but by the same mechanisms they restricted the opportunities of women to receive a formal architectural education. For most of the nineteenth century, architectural training was obtained through office apprenticeships. To be an apprentice involved working within an office and learning skills from other people there; to be an apprentice involved working within a business frame of reference which was considered unsuitable for a lady.

Towards the end of the nineteenth century, architectural schools were founded, mainly in the universities. With this development, aspiring architects could receive their training not only by apprenticing in offices but, with increasing status, through established schools. Many of these new architecture schools emerged from the Morrill Land-Grant act of 1862. The Massachusetts Institute of Technology began in 1868; Cornell University and the University of Illinois were open by 1871. "By 1898 nine schools were actively working with a total enrollment of 362 regular students."[19] By law, Land-Grant universities were open to women and men. But the theory was very different from practice. Few women received architectural degrees in the nineteenth century. Most had to wait another forty years before having the opportunity of studying architecture, and even then, they were not welcome or encouraged. Instead, it was a constant struggle for women to gain admittance. Bertha Yerex Whitman still remembers the biting words of the Dean of Architecture at the University of Michigan when, as a young woman in 1914, she asked to study architecture. He bluntly stated that "we don't want you, but since the school is coeducational and state owned, we have to take you if you insist."[20] This was the attitude of the times; women were looked upon as intruders, not only on the business ladder but in the admission offices of universities as well.

Only under exceptional circumstances, such as the conditions of the Civil War, the worsening plight of the poor in cities that required new forms of social service, or in isolated and revolutionary religious communities, were women given free scope in architecture. However, to enter the profession of architecture officially, to share its domain with men, to have men and women work equally together — these were principles totally contrary to the established social order of the nineteenth century.

In contrast, the American Indian tribes, the pioneers, and the religious communes demonstrated successful alternatives where men and women worked together without a marked distinction made between domestic and public domains. Prizing utility and social unity, their architecture reflected these values in its encompassing concerns. World War I, the Great Depression, and World War II were to bring tremendous changes to American society; with these changes the woman's domain was very slowly transformed and her opportunities to practice architecture expanded.

Footnotes

1. Mrs. Hale, *Manners* (Boston, J. E. Tilton, 1868), p. 21
2. A Lady, *The Young Lady's Friend* (Boston, American Stationers' Company, John B. Russell, 1837), p. 36
3. Mrs. H. O. Ward, *Sensible Etiquette* (Philadelphia, Porter and Coates, 1878), p. 410
4. Mrs. L. H. Sigourney, *Letters To Young Ladies* (Hartford, William Watson, 1835), p. 32
5. Catherine E. Beecher and Harriet Beecher Stowe, *The American Woman's Home* (New York, J. B. Ford and Company, 1869) dedication
6. Agatha Young, *The Women and The Crisis* (New York, Oblensky, 1959), p. 178
7. Kate Gannett Wells, *About People* (Boston, James R. Osgood and Company, 1885), p. 127, 133, 138
8. Sigourney, op. cit., p. 33
9. Cornelia Meigs, *Jane Addams* (Boston, Little, Brown and Company, 1970), p. 144
10. Gerda Lerner, *Black Women in White America* (New York, Vintage Books, 1973), p. 23
11. Ibid, p. 16
12. Ibid, p. 136
13. Ibid, p. 138
14. Charles Nordhoff, *The Communistic Societies of the United States* (New York, Harper and Brothers, Publishers, 1875), p. 412
15. Flo Morse, *Yankee Communes* (New York, Harcourt Brace Jovanovich, Inc., 1971)
16. Edward Deming Andrews, *The People Called Shakers* (New York, Oxford University Press, 1953)
17. A Lady, *The Lady's Companion* (Philadelphia, H. C. Peck & Theo. Bliss, 1852), p. 219
18. Grace Greenwood, *Stories and Sights of France and Italy* (Boston, Ticknor and Fields, 1867), p. 121
19. *Encyclopedia Britannica* (Chicago, Encyclopedia Britannica, Inc., William Benton, Publisher, 1962), volume 2, p. 275
20. Letter from Bertha Yerex Whitman to Doris Cole, January 16, 1972

4 EDUCATION OF WOMEN ARCHITECTS

The Cambridge School

In the fall of 1915 Henry Atherton Frost, a young instructor at the Harvard School of Architecture, was requested by James Sturgis Pray, then head of the Landscape School at Harvard, to tutor a young woman in architectural drafting — since, of course, it was impossible to allow her to study at Harvard. Henry Frost wrote with sympathy and humor that "from the middle of October to Christmastime I met Mr. Pray's young lady two or three afternoons a week in her mother's living room — or did we call it parlor in those days? A card table was set up, the drawing board was hauled out from behind the piano, bright new instruments, T-square, triangles and scale were laid out, and we attacked the classic orders of Vignola, the bible of the architects of the day." But after such an experience, "I had ... decided that tutoring the Tuscan orders on a teetering card table in a lady's parlor produced a certain sense of unreality ... and I had told my student that if she wished to continue, it must be at a solid drafting table in my office where I could drop in every day ... If I had expected this would end it all, and there is no proof that such was my motive, I sadly misjudged the modern young woman of that day." Not only did this young woman accept enthusiastically, but soon there were five other women requesting instruction. Henry Frost and his partner, Bremer Pond, a landscape architect, decided to tutor the five new applicants, but "of course we agreed sternly that this was as far as it would go. We could not let a group of women disrupt our office practice." And so on February 14, 1916, "we had a school and were not aware of it, indeed would have resented the accusation as vigorously as we resented the title of the Frost and Pond Day Nursery conferred upon us by a humorous friend. Indeed the

Henry Atherton Frost, director of the Cambridge School.

term 'school' found favor with the students before it did with us. They began to refer to it as 'the little school'."[1] Thus began the Cambridge School of Architecture and Landscape Architecture, the first and only serious architectural school for women in the United States.

Though women were still confined to the domestic, many educational and social changes were going on during those early years of the twentieth century. "We grew up in a period when women were more and more assuming responsibilities outside their homes. Their struggle for equal suffrage meant simply to us that they wanted to vote, and we, who did not vote if to do so was inconvenient, marvelled at their tenacity." Mr. Frost further explained that "we had no training that helped us to understand that [when founding the Cambridge School] we had quite by chance been caught up in a small eddy of a greater movement in which women were beginning to demand equal educational rights with their brothers."[2]

But the notion of women practicing architecture professionally did not suddenly become an issue in 1915, nor did it preoccupy the minds of women alone. E. C. Gardner, Calvert Vaux, and other men, as well as such women as Harriet Beecher Stowe and Catherine Beecher, had recommended women to the profession of architecture in the nineteenth century, though one must remember the qualification that found women suited for the study of domestic architecture in particular rather than for architecture in general. The great leap from the homely arts to all building types was not even suggested, which is not surprising in light of the nineteenth-century concept of women professionals. This confinement to domestic architecture persisted, without development, even in 1915. That year, when the Cambridge School of Architecture and Landscape Architecture was founded for the education of women, its curriculum was geared for and based upon the firm conviction that women were particularly suited for domestic architecture, and domestic architecture only.

Calvert Vaux found the study of domestic architecture well suited to the feminine nature while, as late as 1928, Henry Frost wrote that "there seemed to be a consensus of opinion that they [women] ... were best suited to do domestic work."[3] Frost also had his eloquent argument for women in domestic architecture.

The two professions of architecture and landscape architecture are peculiarly adapted to women. They are artistic professions such as appeal to the naturally artistic feminine instinct ... the man is likely

to be better in monumental design ... while the woman student has a tendency towards the more delicate side of design, the more intimate scheme. The woman, again, is likely to have a better sense of color and of detail.[4]

Each man certainly meant these thoughts as liberal compliments for women wanting to educate themselves in the profession of domestic architecture. Extending the feminine domain from home management to home design seemed to them a natural and charming idea. In fact, this idyllic image was abhorred by women architects: in it they saw revealed the difficulties of fully practicing their profession even in the existing business world of 1936.

Their [women's] professional work, both in architecture and landscape architecture is likely, though this is by no means always true, to be in domestic fields. The sentimental reasons given for this can be ignored. The true reason is that women practitioners thus far, are more likely to be commissioned by individuals than by corporations and organizations.[5]

Teaching domestic architecture was the objective of Henry Frost and Bremer Pond: it was not the goal of the six women who prevailed upon the liberal ideals of these two men. These women had come to learn everything they could, and they soon stretched the boundaries of the domestic realm to unbelievable frontiers. These first six and the many who followed after them redefined domestic architecture to include schools, hospitals, pavilions, concert halls, country estates, restaurants, modern art centers, and boat clubs, and even to planning and designing entire villages. It was only in 1941 that Henry Frost could admit to the fact that the Cambridge School students were not being taught solely domestic architecture.

A few years ago ... specialization in domestic architecture would have been a satisfactory solution. In these later years, first of depression now of war, the woman student has progressed to a degree which astonishes us who work with her daily. She thinks clearly, reasons well ...[6]

Mr. Frost was delighted with his revelation and with the progress of his students. It was not, however, a revelation to them; they had come to the school to study architecture and "the students led the way, sponsoring new advances. Theirs was the conviction and determination, the vision of changing conditions."[7]

The Cambridge School was established not to teach architecture to women in the passive manner or as only an intellectual pursuit, but to ensure that they could actively practice their profession upon graduation. With this attitude, Mr. Frost took up their cause and "assumed that they are interested in entering these arts only on a strictly professional basis. There are too many poorly trained people in all professions to encourage any other point of view."[8] The School did admit special students who were not working towards a degree, but these women were not encouraged, and the School preferred to increase the number of women seriously directed to professional practice. When possible, the School also accepted women who had not graduated from college and they could earn a Certificate after completing the required curriculum. But from its founding the Cambridge School was essentially a graduate school for women who had previously finished four years of college. The record shows that in the first sixteen years of the School, 72 percent of the students were college graduates, while the remaining 28 percent had qualified for admission through previous study, travel, and office work.[9] They came from forty states, from England, France, Canada, and Mexico, and from forty different colleges.

As a group these women were unusual. Great pains were taken to discourage the hesitant applicant; the hard work, long hours, sacrifices, and existing prejudices were pointed out to the potential student, for Frost knew well what was ahead for them and wanted only those strong in purpose at the Cambridge School.

If in the face of all the discouraging arguments that are presented to her, a woman still persists and is determined to make the necessary sacrifices that hard work entails, the chances are that she will find congenial and attractive work and reasonable opportunities for success.[10]

This policy of realistically appraising all the disadvantages of practicing architecture did seem to be successful in giving those truly interested a chance to study. As of 1930, 83 percent of the graduates were active in professional work, making a very high ratio of more than five-to-one.[11] Considering the record of married graduates alone, there were still 60 percent active professionally. Such statistics reflect changes from cultural patterns of the nineteenth century, and also, perhaps, Mr. Frost's efforts to discourage the uncommitted from attending his school.

Nevertheless the question of marriage was still an issue in 1928, as it had been in the nineteenth century. With only 40 percent of women graduates from six representative architectural schools married, the traditional constraints on women still applied.

In the nineteenth century work outside the home was unthinkable for the married woman ... there were objections from husbands and society to consider. That is why the convinced feminist of the nineteenth century often spurned marriage. Indeed, it is often forgotten that the feminist movement was a form of revolt against marriage ... The tendency [not to marry] was most pronounced, as was to be expected, among highly educated women ... [12]

The difference was that now women like those in the Cambridge School wanted both to marry and to have a professional career. They were interested in finding some reasonable solution towards "the principle of continuity in woman's intellectual, as in her affectional life, as the only condition of her mental health and happiness and the best interests of her family." [13] One of the ways found and practiced by women was to marry architects. The women of the Cambridge School did share projects and parties with their male peers at the Harvard School of Architecture. These activities led to marriages between members of the two schools. Ethel Howes of the Institute of Womens Interests was ecstatic over the "still more inspiring possibilities of married partnerships in the profession ... It is more favorable than even an optimistic view could have foreseen ... here again emerges the general solution of more than one problem; not only that of continuity in individual work ... but that of the pressure of inhibitions against marriage itself, which no woman of tested ability entirely escapes." [14] Marrying an architect increased the likelihood of having a husband who understood and had sympathy for one's work. Marriage to an architect in private practice also solved the need of finding a job, working part-time, and co-ordinating vacations, work schedules, and care of children. The professional marriage that Ethel Howes envisioned was ideal so long as the husband upheld the conviction that architecture was the shared domain of both men and women.

For women who did not have these "married partnerships," there existed the problem of finding architectural offices that would hire them. Henry Frost promised "reasonable opportunities for success,"

The Cambridge School women dressed for a costume party with the Harvard School of Design, circa 1924.

but as a practicing architect, he knew the frustrations and difficulties of this most exacting profession even for men, and wrote that "success comes usually from keeping everlastingly at a thing . . . if such a statement is true for men, it is equally true for women." He understood, however, that female students suffered special handicaps, for "as in all other professions, there seems to be some doubt as to just what women can do in professional work. There is still prejudice on the part of more conservative men . . . and even in many of the co-educational schools . . ."

Though Mr. Frost attributed these doubts to "conservative men," he himself did not escape these prejudices and doubts concerning the abilities of female professionals. In a study for the Institute for Co-ordination of Womens Interests in 1928 he wrote that "women seem to be as yet not as creative in their design work as men are, [but] this does not indicate that woman is not without value in an office." Despite his doubts about women's creative ability, he saw other avenues open to them; he very accurately explained that "in the offices design, while still of importance, is more dependent upon those who excel in construction, in writing of specifications, in the ability to estimate costs and returns and other practical matters

"Without a knowledge of how things are put together good design is impossible and cannot be put into execution."
H. A. Frost

which the student is likely to scorn." Unfortunately "there seemed to be a consensus of opinion that they [women] were not as able to do work in engineering and construction as men." And he further observed that "people are apt to be skeptical as to the ability of women to do work, especially that requiring knowledge of engineering and construction details, and their ability to deal with contractors and workmen."[15] It was not surprising that in the face of such criticism and doubts "women as a rule seem to prefer to work on what they can handle and supervise in detail themselves."

Though Mr. Frost expressed reservations in his writings, his actions did not reflect these doubts. Not only did he place women graduates in offices, but he had a woman partner, Eleanor Raymond, from 1919 to 1935. During this period, while his energies were directed more and more to the Cambridge School, she took over much of the responsibility for the practice. As of 1930, 34 percent of Cambridge School graduates were in independent practice or were associates or partners in architectural firms; 39 percent were draftswomen in offices; and 10 percent were in education, lecturing, or editorial work.[16]

Though such achievements were in some respects remarkable, they certainly do not indicate that obtaining work was easy for these women. For one thing, the doubts and prejudices of society affected the type of work available to women. According to a 1936 bulletin of the Cambridge School, "women practitioners thus far, are more likely to be commissioned by individuals than by corporations and organizations."[17] Women, when educated, were educated with other women, and their contact was largely with their servants, children, and families; though in a profession which depended largely upon personal contacts for commissions, they did not have contact with the male hierarchies of corporations.

Another trend affecting the practice of architecture was specialization. Even in 1928, Frost noted that offices were beginning to specialize in particular building types — hospitals, schools, municipal

Following pages:
Sculptor's Studio in Dover, Massachusetts, by Eleanor Raymond, 1933.

Ms. Raymond was one of the first women to study architecture at the Cambridge School. From 1919 to 1935 she practiced architecture with Mr. Frost; in 1935 she opened an independent office; during World War II she was head of the drafting room at the Radar School of the Massachusetts Institute of Technology; and was honored by the American Institute of Architects by being elected to its College of Fellows in 1961.

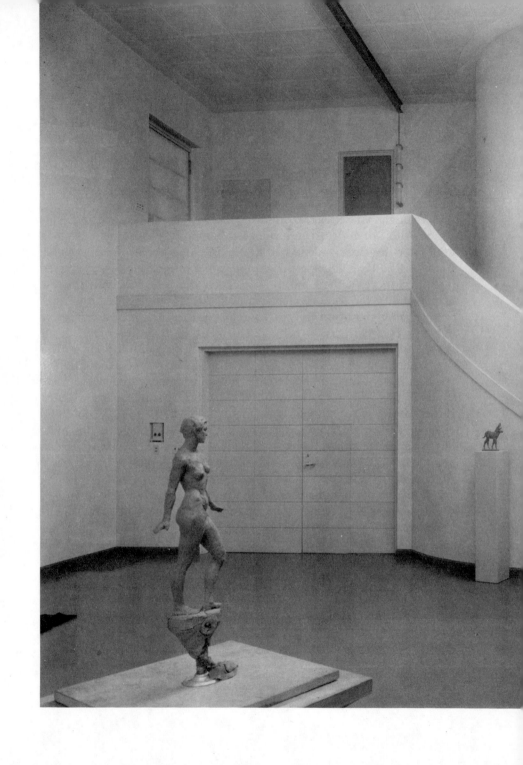

buildings, or domestic architecture. He noted that "in both architecture and landscape architecture the modern tendency towards specialization offers little chance for the jack-of-all trades and the general practitioner is disappearing." Collaboration replaced the individual's highly personal style in design, and large, compartmentalized offices replaced the small, loosely organized firms. Women in independent practice usually had small offices and, as noted, had difficulty in attracting corporate clients; with the trend toward complexity, they were further pushed into the corner of domestic architecture. The alternative for women was to enter larger offices. To do this they had to gain acceptance by the men who ran them. As shown through records of the Cambridge School graduates, an attempt was made by working as associates, partners, and draftswomen in architectural firms, and by becoming the wives and thereby the partners of practicing male architects.

Like most architects, Henry Frost was concerned with improving public taste and clients' willingness to accept the forms of modern architecture, which were just beginning to appear in the United States. At that time the classical orders were still the style not only in buildings but in the curriculum of schools, and the architectural profession, dependent upon clients and conditioned to serve their aesthetic preferences, could not exist without the consent and encouragement of the public. Henry Frost did not except women from the responsibilities of trying to educate the public, and he actually placed great hope on the influence that they could exert. "The personal contacts that well trained women are in a position to make should prove to be an important factor in raising the standards required by the public."[18] Realistically, however, the hundred or so women who had received degrees by 1936 could not have achieved this goal. But they were successful out of all proportion to their numbers. They spread the message of their work from Massachusetts to California to Tennessee to Maryland. In each place their buildings, though not always modern, were responsible and exemplary architecture. That is not to say that Cambridge School graduates were not innovative in their work; the magazine *Architectural Forum* of 1933 published what they termed the first modern house in Massachusetts by one of them, Eleanor Raymond. The School's graduates had the "enthusiasm of youth and conservatism of maturity [that] mixed in proper proportions assure a progress from which there will be no need to turn back."[19]

The summer school of the Cambridge School in Rockport, Massachusetts.

Aside from professional practice, these women architects were strong supporters of the Cambridge School. Many gave scholarships and donations to encourage and provide opportunity to more women desiring careers in architecture and landscape architecture. The large building at 53 Church Street in Cambridge was given to the School by one of its supporters. Another donated the use of a house in Rockport on Cape Ann for summer sessions.

Henry Frost was considered by the women of the Cambridge School to be an inspiring teacher. This opinion did not come from women who were inexperienced in the qualities of teachers, for the students at the School had, in general, completed four years at some of the finest colleges. Besides a liberal arts background he advocated a three-year graduate course, travel and study in Europe, and apprenticeship. Not only did he advocate this training, but he provided most of these items within the curriculum of the Cambridge School.

The staff, often young architects just starting their careers, grew from a very few in 1915 to over fifteen in 1936. Some of these teachers worked full-time at the School, but many came from the Harvard Graduate School of Design and similar institutions, or else were in private practice in the Boston area. Aside from this regular teaching staff, there were special critics and guest lectures brought

91

in throughout the school year. As in all architectural schools, the courses and faculty were diversified at the Cambridge School. Such people as Stephen Hamblin from the Lexington Botanical Gardens, Frank Rines of the Massachusetts School of Art, and Bracett K. Thorogood, educational counselor at Franklin Union, gave courses there, and the record shows that many notable men and women architects began their teaching careers at the school — Freda Gilfillan, Mary Cunningham, Ethel Power, G. Holmes Perkins, Walter Bogner, and Edith Cochran were just a few of the many instructors. Henry Frost wrote to William Neilson about the Cambridge School in 1939, "G. Holmes Perkins and Marc Peter, Jr., both of whom are lecturers in your Graduate School of Architecture, are among the ten competitors who have placed in the preliminary competition for the new Smithsonian Institute. I thought you would be interested to know that we have some good instructors here."[20]

The course of study offered at the Cambridge School was similar to the curriculum at other schools of its day. There were three major divisions — design, construction, and freehand drawing. Within these

"A person to whom wealth is the sole end of effort does not choose the professional life."
H. A. Frost

Pillsbury Residence in Duxbury, Massachusetts, by Sarah Harkness, 1942.

Ms. Harkness received her architectural degree from the Cambridge School in 1938. In 1945 Sarah and John Harkness, along with five other young architects, joined Walter Gropius to form The Architects Collaborative. This architectural firm has grown from eight in 1946 to over two hundred in 1973, doing work throughout the United States and in many foreign countries.

three divisions were such courses as architectural and landscape design, construction (working drawings and details), history, plant materials, mathematics, graphics, and sketching. The students were required to take and demonstrate proficiency in all these courses. The School realized that "architecture and landscape architecture are professions combining requirements of design, technical understanding and business acumen. A perfect balance of such widely divergent qualities is not to be expected in any individual."[21] But, like other architectural schools, it aspired to this "perfect balance."

Collaboration and co-operation between the related disciplines were dominant points in Henry Frost's professional philosophy and were practiced at the Cambridge School of Architecture and Landscape Architecture throughout its existence. "It has always been, so far as I know, the only school maintaining a close relation between architecture and landscape architecture under one faculty requiring of its landscape students a considerable amount of architectural training."[22] Not only were landscape students given training in architecture, but architectural students were given training in landscaping. This interdisciplinary education began when the School taught mainly domestic architecture and continued when it expanded in scope to include all building types.

Only much later, in the 1940s, after the Cambridge School closed and women were admitted to the Harvard Graduate School of Design, did Harvard stress the relationship between architecture and landscape architecture. This change at Harvard was partly due to Henry Frost, who continued teaching at Harvard and advocating the cross pollination of the two professions. In 1943, while still corresponding with the former Cambridge School alumnae, he happily reported that "the collaboration between architecture and landscape architecture has been strengthened to a degree satisfactory to even its most enthusiastic sponsors. It would seem to me to possess now most of the virtues we so firmly approved of in the Cambridge School . . ."[23] Thus the collaborative education begun by Henry Frost and the Cambridge School in 1915 was finally adopted by Harvard University in 1942.

At the Cambridge School of Architecture and Landscape Architecture the two professions were integrated in curriculum throughout the entire three-and-a-half-year course of study. "A student electing either of these programs is required to take a certain amount of work in the other, on the theory that an architect should know something of the principles of landscape architecture; a landscape architect, something of the principles of architecture."[24] In common with other architectural schools of that time, as well as schools today, design was considered the most important course at the Cambridge School. What was unusual at the Cambridge School was that in the

112 Charles Street in Boston by Eleanor Raymond, 1923.

The educational philosophy and training of the Cambridge School emphasized the co-ordination of architecture with landscape architecture.

94

design studios the basic course was the same for both the architectural and landscape students; and during the intermediate and advanced design courses half of the problems were the same for both groups. It was only at the technical level of detail that the training divided, with the landscapers concentrating on plant materials and plant design while the aspiring architects studied professional practice, heating, and plumbing and structural systems. The art history classes and freehand drawing studios were also combined for the two programs; this collaborative education did influence the professional approach of Cambridge School graduates. The works of Eleanor Raymond and Gertrude Sawyer, among others, show that landscape design has been a natural feature of their architecture.

During the first year of study at the Cambridge School, an additional summer term was required of all students. Where and how this summer term was taught varied through the years. In 1932 a generous alumna offered the School the use of her house on Cape Ann, Massachusetts. Off one side of the drafting room was a box garden and apple trees, while the other side of the house opened to a view of green lawn, apple orchards, and the ocean. This idyllic setting was "cooled by a fountain that carries one back to Italian gardens."[25] Unfortunately, the house was no longer made available to the Cambridge School after 1939. At this point in its history the School negotiated a joint summer school with Harvard to be held at Robinson Hall. The Cambridge School suffered a loss of income, since the income from the summer session went to Harvard, and lost as well direct control over its students.

Another feature of the Cambridge School was travel and study in Europe. These trips were by no means reverent pilgrimages to view the monuments of antiquity. Mr. Frost sagely observed that "in every age when struggles for existence and for governmental solidarity have passed on to economic well being, new and important edifices have arisen differing from those of former periods."[26] It was with this attitude that he showed past and present architecture to his student travelers.

Apprenticeship was the final item on Frost's list of requirements for a proper architectural training. However, as much as he advised women to work in large offices and "assumed that they are interested in entering these arts only on a strictly professional basis,"[27] there seemed to be no organized plan for implementing this desired apprenticeship in architectural firms. Some graduates worked for Mr.

Frost and Mr. Pond; others found job openings in schools such as Smith College and Northwestern University. As the record shows in 1930, with 83 percent of them active in professional work, Cambridge School graduates seemed to find employment by one means or another.

Reacting to the growing complexity of society in the United States, Henry Frost expanded his educational goals in accordance with professional needs. He found the Cambridge School woman capable of handling the new challenges: in 1941, he wrote that "she thinks clearly, reasons well, and is interested in housing rather than houses; in community centers for the masses rather than in neighborhood clubs for the elect; in regional planning more than in estate planning; in social aspects of her profession more than in private commissions." He had praise for her ability when he noted that "she is intelligent. She coordinates her work well, collaborates with others successfully ... the woman student has progressed to a degree which astonishes us." He observed that "her interest in her profession embraces its

"The woman student has progressed to a degree which astonishes us who work with her daily."
H. A. Frost

social and human implications." Realizing this growth in ability and interest, Henry Frost proposed a new and expanded program for the degree of Master of Architecture at the Cambridge School. He proposed "that the year or longer required for the Master's degree both in architecture and in landscape architecture should be one of research and design in the direction of (for want of a better term) socialized architecture." As always, he was thinking in terms of practicing a profession, and he felt that this program would "fit them, perhaps as no other school does at present, for positions of responsibility on the planning boards of cities and towns, and in other organizations having to do with social welfare." He wanted them during this year or more of study to "come in contact with innumerable organizations and individuals engaged in planning for the future of our communities" and to "present to them real rather than hypothetical problems." He gave credit where it was due when he wrote that the idea, "started undoubtedly with the students themselves, was recognized and has been encouraged by the faculty in the types of problems given them." Unfortunately, this expanded Master's program was never put into effect at the Cambridge School, for only one year later the School was closed permanently. And with the closing of the School there passed the opportunity to begin a program which would have been "in step with the spirit of the times and may be so organized as to serve the future."[28]

Though the Cambridge School for women was incorporated in 1924 under Massachusetts law, it had only the authority to grant certificates to its graduates. These certificates had been sufficient in the past for the practice of architecture but, as government control was more formulated, the Cambridge School needed the ability to grant the professional degrees which had become necessary, in many states, for those who wished to practice architecture. Therefore, the trustees and the Director chose to seek out an accredited women's college for affiliation. In Frost's report of 1928, he pointed out that "there is one advantage that we lose permanently if we become part of a women's college. At some time . . . we shall want to make the School co-educational. This would be impossible as a graduate school of a women's college."[29] Unhappily, he did not also foresee the loss of independence and self-determination through affiliation, and it was this loss which was later to become the critical one for the School.

With affiliation in mind, Frost wrote to President William Neilson of Smith College in 1928, asking his opinion of a collaborative affiliation with several women's colleges. Neilson replied that he was not very hopeful over the possibilities of a collaborative scheme. Nevertheless, he was very interested in having the Cambridge School as an affiliate of Smith College. The arrangements progressed slowly, while the Cambridge School tried to clear its constant debt; the Trustees of Smith College voted affirmatively on the affiliation in the spring of 1932.

As the affiliation progressed, the Cambridge School, its assets and liabilities, became part of Smith College. In 1938 the books of the Cambridge School were closed, and Smith became the official owner of the School. From that time, the School was known as "Smith College, Graduate School of Architecture and Landscape Architecture, Formerly The Cambridge School." Part of this agreement allowed the continuing location of the School in Cambridge, Massachusetts, and, naturally, Henry Frost remained its Director and driving force.

With this affiliation and eventual ownership by Smith College, the Cambridge School gained the power to grant official degrees. Two types were awarded: Certificates in Architecture or Landscape Architecture to women who completed the three-and-a-half-year program but who did not already hold Bachelor of Arts or Science degrees from accredited colleges, and graduate degrees of Bachelor of Architecture or Landscape Architecture to women who had completed the same program and had already earned Bachelor of Arts or Science degrees at four-year colleges. The School also awarded the degrees of Master of Architecture or Landscape Architecture to those students who had completed an additional one to one-and-a-half-year course after earning the Bachelor of Architecture or Landscape Architecture. The B.Arch., BLA, M.Arch., and MLA were similar to the type of degrees then being offered at the Harvard Graduate School of Design and other graduate architectural schools.

But the happy and sympathetic relationship between Frost and Neilson was soon to end. President Neilson retired in the spring of 1939. Little did anyone realize that with the retirement of Neilson, the very life of the Cambridge School was to be affected. It was Neilson and his ideal of making Smith College a university that had resulted in acquisition of the Cambridge School; it was his sympathy and understanding that encouraged Frost in future plans for the School and supported him through numerous economic crises. Without Neilson, the relation between Smith College and the Cambridge School changed, and only three years later the Cambridge School closed.

This change in relations with Smith College can be seen during the twenty-fifth year celebration of the Cambridge School for women. Frost, of course, invited the Acting President of Smith, Mrs. D. W. Morrow, and explained that they were "staging an exhibition on Houses and Housing which is quite the most ambitious thing we have attempted. It will be at the Hotel Somerset from March first through March fourth."[30] Henry Frost received an answer not from Mrs. Morrow but from her secretary, saying that "she wishes me to express to you her appreciation of the invitation and her regret at having to miss what promises to be a pleasant occasion."[31] Perhaps to call "the most ambitious thing we have attempted" only a "pleasant occasion" was the fault of the secretary and not of the Acting President, but this discrepancy of view was symbolic of the events to follow.

The Exhibition of Houses and Housing covered the large Princess Ballroom at the Hotel Somerset in Boston. Aside from the main exhibit, the architectural instructors at the School showed their own work. Included was the work of G. Holmes Perkins, Walter Bogner, Marc Peter, and Hugh Stubbins. The exhibit was organized by the Museum of Modern Art of New York, and during the four days of this exhibit, there were also lectures by Mrs. Walter Gropius and Miss Cynthia Wiley. It was a great success, with 825 persons visiting the exhibition in four days. The twenty-five-year celebration and exhibition was successful in every aspect except the financial. Not only was little money raised for the School, but extra money had to be spent on the celebration itself.

In September 1940 Herbert J. Davis took over the presidency of Smith College. Only one year passed before President Davis clearly and strongly warned Henry Frost of the tenuous position for the future life of the Cambridge School. And he quite frankly reported the Trustees' disinterest in continuing the School with any additional financial cost to Smith College.

I am much afraid that unless we can substantially reduce the present deficit the Trustees will decide to give up the school at the earliest possible moment, and I think you ought to know of this danger and take it into account in connection with all proposals for added expense.[32]

Gone were the days of sympathetic support from President Neilson; gone, too, were the days of his constant begging for funds for his graduate schools. The trustees wanted balanced budgets, facts, and figures — not the grander dreams of Frost and Neilson. They were ready to abandon the School "at the earliest possible moment," and this was exactly what they did just two months later.

In the winter of 1941, conditions were indeed precarious for the United States. The country was at war, and the thoughts and energies of the American people were necessarily turned towards this calamity. Each day more young men were leaving their work and their studies for the front. It was not the time for the Smith College Trustees to have sympathy for visions like those of the Cambridge School with its budgetary liabilities.

War conditions also had their direct impact on Harvard's Graduate School of Design. It was dependent upon young men to fill its enrollment, and these young men were leaving for war. According to Henry Frost, at this point "President Conant [of Harvard] has told Mr. Hudnut that he is willing to propose the admission of women to the School of Design."[33] Women were to be allowed to study architecture and landscape architecture at the Harvard Graduate School of Design. But even this acceptance was not wholehearted, as "Dean Hudnut, while he believes that once women are admitted to the School of Design, the arrangement will be permanent, will of course announce it as for the period of the war." Even "Mr. Gropius, who has been, of course, the chief instigator of the admission of women to the Harvard School, suggested tentatively that they be admitted as special students and not as candidates for the Harvard degree."

Throughout these negotiations, Henry Frost, as usual, thought first of the welfare of his students. The idea that the students should not be candidates for degrees at Harvard was "not to be thought of, and if his [Mr. Gropius'] suggestion should be accepted — as I have no reason to believe it would be — it would become necessary for us here to advise our students to go elsewhere than to Harvard."[34] In the end, Harvard did accept women as candidates for degrees. The plans were finalized and the announcement was made to the Cambridge School women on February 4, 1942. The official reason for closing the Cambridge School was "to avoid wherever possible unnecessary duplication in educational programs."[35] Of course, this arrangement, which was "for the duration of the war," was in reality forever.

The Cambridge School closed, but its enthusiastic students continued their education at Harvard with the extremely large registration of twenty-eight women. Henry Frost continued to teach architecture at Harvard and could follow the progress of his former students. This progress he noted in his newsletter, "The Cambridge School at Harvard," to alumnae and friends. Frost was an optimist and wanted to believe that "the final transition this spring from a collaboration of interests to a unity of effort, [was] an entirely natural step."[36] In 1942, with twenty-eight women enrolled in architecture, it was impossible to see the future, to see that only ten years later the enrollment of women would be cut in half. Frost in 1943 could "look back one year to the time when the School of Design announced the admission of women, and to remember some of the scathing comments of Harvard alumni. What was then considered a special concession . . . has become in twelve short months a general policy for undergraduate courses. . ."[37] At the war effort increased, the number of young men decreased, and Harvard began to look more and more like a school for women. The former Cambridge School students were quite capable of doing the work assigned to them, and Frost proudly noted the high grades achieved by these women. They not only helped Harvard to survive the war years and fulfilled the academic standards of this institution, but they were equally successful in "upholding the Cambridge School tradition valiantly."[38]

But the Cambridge School of Architecture and Landscape Architecture was dead, killed by unbalanced budgets, war, changing times, and the needs of Harvard's architectural school to fill its ranks. Left behind were the cries of those who mourned its passing. To Frost and many of the alumnae, "the peremptory closing of the School in Cambridge was in the nature of a tragedy."[39] Letters, petitions, and telegrams of protest filled the office of the President of Smith College. "We face the end of a period. For some of us it means possibly a farewell to the best part of our lives, to a period of fine adventure . . ."[40] The "fine adventure," the Cambridge School, was gone.

But why mourn the passing of this institution? Harvard University had accepted women, and now other architectural schools as well were accepting them. What need was there for a women's school? "The time had come in our civilization when universities must be co-educational at the graduate school level. Women must have the same rights as men ... "[41] As it has turned out, however, the fears of women concerning their educational opportunities were more than justified.

Women were indeed admitted to universities and, at least at Harvard, there were few policies of discrimination. But where are the women architects who continue the proud and brave traditions of the Cambridge School women? There are shockingly few women architects practicing in this country today or studying in its professional schools. The end of the Cambridge School marked "the end of an era." It was to be greatly mourned, and rightfully so because as an institution it not only educated women but encouraged them, prodded them, pulled from them their dormant potential.

It is obvious, too, that the closing of the Cambridge School blunted the sword of one of the few champions of women architects, Henry Frost. Without him the School might never have survived as long as it did. Frost liked teaching women; he believed in their ability; he thought only of their interests. No group, institution, or person has replaced Henry Frost; there is no champion for women architects today.

The idea of a school of architecture solely for women is perhaps out of date, nor was it the final aim of the Cambridge School. But the School's aim of encouraging women in architecture is still an issue and a dream that has not been fulfilled. Henry Atherton Frost's words still apply thirty years later. He wrote then: "One thing this School has stood for in its twenty-five years is to break down discrimination against women in education. It seems necessary to continue to do so."[42]

Footnotes

1. Henry Atherton Frost, autobiographical manuscript — unpublished, 1943, p. 6, 8
2. Ibid, p. 8
3. Henry Atherton Frost and William R. Sears, *Women In Architecture and Landscape Architecture*, A Study for the Institute for the Co-ordination of Womens Interests, Publication #7 (Northampton, Mass., Smith College, 1928), p. 26
4. Ibid, p. 24
5. "The Cambridge School of Architecture and Landscape Architecture" An affiliated Graduate Professional School of Smith College, 53 Church Street, Cambridge, Mass., 1936
6. letter from Henry Frost to Herbert Davis, June 20, 1941, p. 3
7. "The Cambridge School of Architecture and Landscape Architecture" op. cit.
8. Frost and Sears, op. cit.
9. "The Cambridge School for Domestic Architecture and Landscape Architecture" Bulletin #23, 53 Church Street at Harvard Square, Cambridge, Mass., February 1930
10. Frost and Sears, op. cit.
11. 'The Cambridge School for Domestic Architecture and Landscape Architecture" Bulletin #23, op. cit.
12. *Daedalus, The Woman In America*, Spring 1964, Carl N. Degler, "Revolution without Ideology: The Changing Place of Women in America," p. 666
13. Ethel Howes, "Introduction," *Women In Architecture and Landscape Architecture*, A Study for the Institute for Co-ordination of Womens Interests, Publication #7 (Northampton, Mass., Smith College, 1928)
14. Ibid
15. Frost and Sears, op. cit.
16. "The Cambridge School for Domestic Architecture and Landscape "Architecture" Bulletin #23, op. cit.
17. "The Cambridge School of Architecture and Landscape Architecture" Cambridge, Mass., 1936, op. cit.
18. Frost and Sears, op. cit.
19. "The Cambridge School of Architecture and Landscape Architecture" Cambridge, Mass., 1936, op. cit.
20. letter from Henry Frost to William Neilson, May 15, 1939
21. "The Cambridge School of Architecture and Landscape Architecture" Cambridge, Mass., 1936

22. "A Report to the Trustees of the Cambridge School," made by the Director, October 25, 1928, p. 5
23. "The Cambridge School at Harvard," June 7, 1943
24. "The Cambridge School of Domestic Architecture and Landscape Architecture," Bulletin #10, The Faculty and Courses for the Year 1923-24, 13 Boylston Street, Cambridge, Mass.
25. "Brochure on Summer School," 1932
26. Frost and Sears, op. cit., p. 20
27. Ibid
28. letter from Henry Frost to Herbert Davis, June 20, 1941
29. "A Report to the Trustees of the Cambridge School" made by the Director, October 25, 1928, p. 8
30. letter from Henry Frost to Mrs. Dwight W. Morrow, January 8, 1940
31. letter from Amillia Clark to Henry Frost, January 10, 1940
32. letter from Herbert Davis to Henry Frost, November 28, 1941
33. letter from Henry Frost to Herbert Davis, January 15, 1942
34. Ibid
35. "To the Students," February 4, 1942
36. Henry Frost, "The Cambridge School at Harvard," December 1942
37. Henry Frost, "The Cambridge School at Harvard," June 7, 1943
38. Henry Frost, "The Cambridge School at Harvard," December 1942
39. "The Cambridge School of Smith College," Architecture and Landscape Architecture, Alumnae Bulletin, Volume XIV, Number 2, July 1942
40. Ibid
41. Ibid
42. letter from Henry Frost to Herbert Davis, January 15, 1942

5 CONTEMPORARY PRACTICE

The Role of Women Architects

The early graduates from the Cambridge School of Architecture and Landscape Architecture and their colleagues from other schools presented clearly the picture of female architects before World War II. They were residential architects doing large and small houses for private clients. As late as 1948, when the *Architectural Record* did a series of articles entitled "A Thousand Women in Architecture," it found that "women architects show a preponderance of domestic architecture."[1] The magazine presented women from all sectors of the country — Delaware; New York; Washington, D. C.; California; Alabama; Michigan; Minnesota; Texas. In each case, and in each sector of the country, though women architects did do other types of projects, the majority of their work was domestic. The *Architectural Record* explained "it is natural that residential architecture should be their particular forte as traditionally and through long experience they are familiar with the problems of creating a better environment for the family."[2] Here the magazine reflected quite unconsciously the prevailing social attitudes, which had effectively confined women to the home and limited the scope of their architectural practice.

As the previous chapters document, many women architects were not satisfied with the restrictions to domestic architecture. They

Oxley Hall, dormitory for women, at Ohio State University, by Florence Rector, 1908.

Florence Kenyon Hayden Rector was the first licensed woman architect in Ohio. Mrs. Rector's mother, who had seen the fate of many Southern women after the Civil War, encouraged her daughters to educate themselves for professional careers. Florence Rector not only had an active architectural practice but was a worker for woman suffrage and was financial chairwoman of the National Women's Party in 1921.

yearned to try their skills at all building types, to tackle a variety of architectural problems; though this objective was present in the early 1900s, it was not fully implemented until the 1940s and the Second World War. This war provided women with expanded opportunities to study architecture, and it also provided them with the opportunity to expand the variety of their architectural projects. As with previous wars involving the United States, women were encouraged to contribute to the war effort through their work. They went to the factories, offices, and governmental bureaus, taking upon themselves the tasks of the absent men. Margaret Van Pelt Vilas attended courses in tool design at Yale and then took a job as tool designer in a war plant; Elisabeth Coit took a War Emergency Appointment with the Federal Public Housing Authority; Juliet Alice Peddle worked on George Field at Vincennes for Miller and Yeager architects; Freda Gilfillan was a ship draftswoman.[3] Women proved themselves, once again, to be capable of meeting these varied demands and, just as after the previous wars, they were unwilling to retreat to the domestic domain once the crisis had ended. The nation was changed by the Second World War, and with it women's concept of themselves; this, of course, led in time to a different status for women architects.

The expansion of women into the labor force necessitated by the demands of the Second World War has continued through the decades following. It is now no longer unusual or shocking for a woman to work, no matter what her family background might be. Today 49 percent of women in the United States are part of the labor force, though most of these women still hold positions of lower rank and pay.[4] Women have progressed from domestic to civic activities, to "female" occupations such as social work, teaching, and nursing, to practically all existing occupations. It is in the past twenty years that women have entered the areas which society — including both men and women — has considered to be "unfeminine." Though the numbers are few, women are now found in nearly all businesses and professions. Twenty years, however, is a relatively short time span, and women, and women architects, have not yet fully defined their place in the working world.

Today, women still practice domestic architecture, but now they handle building projects of all types as well. Their projects now include large-scale residential developments, office buildings, schools, churches, hospitals, airports, hotels, and every conceivable building type. Lucille Raport, president of Compstad, Inc., in California, is

Housing study by Elizabeth Coit, 1965.

Since receiving her degree in 1919, Miss Coit has devoted most of her career to housing designed for low-income families. She is a Fellow of the American Institute of Architects; earned the A.I.A. Langley Award in 1937-39 for housing studies; was Principal Project Planner in Design Department, N.Y.C. Housing Authority from 1942 to 1962; and organized first course of lectures and demonstrations in home repairs for American Women's Voluntary Services.

planning a 3,500-acre recreation and wildlife park; Emily Obst reports that "last year [1971] I was appointed by Governor Askew to be supervising architect for Palm Beach and Okeechobee counties for the Division of Hotels and Restaurants ... I am also working with Non-Profit Housing Inc., an association of 36 religious organizations dedicated to low cost housing in Palm Beach County"; Anne Tennent finds that her practice in North Carolina includes "apartments, banks, stores, light industrial ... and major remodeling work to Salisbury

City Offices, Rowan County Courthouse and Rowan County Community Building."[5] This variety of building types is typical for most women presently practicing architecture.

The most striking characteristic of contemporary women architects is the diversity of their professional lives and work. There is diversity in their geographical locations, education, motivations, work patterns, projects, interests, and professional goals. Of course, there is diversity among all architects, both men and women, but this characteristic is more apparent among women perhaps because there are so few or perhaps because these few had to be so flexible to survive within the established profession. Each woman's career is greatly influenced by her personal life situation, children, marriage, family obligations, and job opportunities — all of which reflect national, economic, and social trends. But in all cases, the desire to practice is strong and, therefore, flexibility is necessary.

The present geographical location of women architects follows a pattern similar to that of the profession in general. Women are scattered throughout the country, from Alaska to Florida. In heavily populated states, such as New York and California, one finds the greatest number of architects, and the greatest concentration of female architects. In Alaska, 4 percent of the resident registered architects are women (that is to say, two of the total forty-four), and Florida lists 7 percent. The count dips to zero for women architects in Nebraska, South Dakota, Nevada, and Idaho, while Iowa, South Carolina, Arkansas, Minnesota, and many others do little better. Both Massachusetts and Texas hold approximately thirty female resident registered architects, which makes them highest after California and New York. In most states, about 1 percent of resident architects are female, the numbers varying with the architectural population.[6]

The motivations for entering the profession of architecture are varied for each woman, but an intense interest in the field is common to all of them. Architecture is a combination of art, technology, the

Old Harbor Village, the first low cost public housing built in Boston, was by Eleanor Manning O'Connor, 1937.

Ms. O'Connor was active professionally from her graduation from M.I.T. in 1906 until July 1973 when she died in Mexico while doing research on Indian cultures. Her career was long and productive, but unfortunately little of her work has been documented. Eleanor Manning O'Connor is one example among many for the need of documenting the work of women architects before all records are lost.

social sciences, and business; and an initial interest in at least one of the fields has led most women into architecture. One woman wrote, "I majored in art, and progressed to architecture, the 'Father of all Arts.' I looked for a challenge that would consume me for all eternity, and found it in architecture." Many of these women were encouraged by their families: "I never felt that I was being educated . . . in order to prepare myself for a 'good' marriage. I was supposed to be Something — a scientist, a professor, a musician — a somebody with a title. Actually, when I came home one day from high school and announced that I had decided to be an Architect they [my parents] took the news gravely and respectfully."[7]

There are few generalizations which can be formed concerning the current work patterns of women architects. Their architectural educations have led them to a variety of occupations — Marie C. Turner (MIT, B.S. in architecture 1909) and her sister have written three books on peddler dolls and are now constructing a doll-house like the old Camp Ground houses of the 1870s found on Martha's Vineyard;[8] Florence Luscomb (MIT, B.S. in architecture 1909) has devoted her life to political reform, being termed "the very model of a modern revolutionary" by *Time* magazine in 1971.[9] Still other women use their architectural training within the profession as single practitioners, married partners, office employees, governmental workers, teachers, and writers. As single practitioners they generally head small offices. As partners they usually work with their husbands. As office employees, they are valued workers but rarely rise to a high position within the office hierarchy. In general, they do poorly in the corporate structure and seldom attain the trappings of professional prestige.

In their practice of architecture women have involved themselves in all its phases — programing, design, working drawings, specifications, field supervision, client contact, and administration. Their status as draftswomen or job captains has depended not only upon their skills, but the opportunities open to women within the office structure. Since much of the time spent within an office is involved with producing the contract documents, women have often devoted a great part of their time to this production. But contrary to professional myth, an inborn bent for intricate detail work was not reported by any of the women interviewed. These women also noted few problems with field supervision, and many actually expressed their enjoyment in the process of construction, finding that once the relationship

William Randolph Hearst's San Simeon in California by Julia Morgan, 1919.

Miss Morgan received a degree in civil engineering at University of California Berkeley in 1894 and later studied at the Ecole in Paris. She was the protegee and sometime associate of architect Bernard Maybeck. The News Report of *Architecture West* reports that "she returned with an ability to work in any style — not with Maybeck's flair for drama but with decorum and generosity. Her numerous women's clubs and YWCA's dignified women's search for individuality early in the century; her redwood houses in Berkeley are squarish and informally elegant. But she is best known for her churches and her buildings at Mills College. How she submerged herself in the demands of the master of San Simeon is puzzling."

is established and the contractor recovers from his surprise, the working relation is a happy one based on mutual respect.[10]

Contemporary women architects have been educated in school and trained at the office to do the same work as their male colleagues. As one female architect put it, "if a woman is going to perform a man's work, she must be more capable than a man doing the same task."[11]

"This is the crew which for many years decided the type, the size, and the location of every bridge in the state of Ohio over twenty foot span."
Josephine E. Powers

After receiving her architectural degree from Columbia University, Miss Powers opened an office with Miss Marion Hindman in 1931 at Columbus, Ohio. Later she became connected with the bridge bureau of the State Highway Department supervising and designing all architectural matters related to their bridge program.

Most women architects are still trying to prove their ability to work at "man's task," believing that this is the proper means of gaining equal status and is the proper goal for female architects. Charles W. Ferguson explained in *The Male Attitude* that contemporary education perpetuates this outlook.

The creature who finishes the curriculum in our schools and colleges is thoroughly indoctrinated in male traditions and methods and values and is bound to speak from the male point of view, whether he (or she) knows it or acknowledges it.[12]

But for some women architects, proving their capability is no longer the question — their emphasis has shifted to examining the profession itself. Women's social consciousness, their desire to serve those in need, and their appreciation for functional requirements have again found expression in their criticism of architectural goals and practices.

Activity among women in architecture and the related disciplines began as early as 1893 with the Chicago World's Fair; in the Woman's Building designed by Sophia Hayden (MIT, B.S. in architecture 1890) were large murals by Mary Cassatt and Mary MacMonnies depicting modern and primitive woman, and displays describing women's work and interests. Even at this early date the organizer, Sara Hallowell, firmly believed that such a display should reflect women's goals, not female ability to perform "men's tasks."[13] In 1921 Elizabeth Martini formed the Chicago Drafting Club, which later became known as the Women's Architectural Club; it included architects, draftswomen, renderers, landscape architects, and architectural students. This group of women met regularly for discussions and lectures, organized displays for the Woman's World Fairs of 1927 and 1928, sponsored an International Exhibition of women in architecture and the allied arts at Century of Progress (Chicago, 1933), and held their own exhibition featuring the work of professional women such as Ruth Perkins, Bertha Yerex Whitman, and Elizabeth Kimball Nedved.[14] Also, in 1922 the Association of Women in Architecture was formed, soon totaling twelve undergraduate chapters and nine professional chapters whose purpose was "to promote mutual encouragement, friendship, and the exchange of ideas among women with common interests and ideals in the fields of architecture."[15] But unfortunately, with the passing years, interest lagged as few women

Following pages:
The Woman's Building at Columbian Exposition in Chicago by Sophia Hayden, 1893.

Ms. Hayden received her architectural degree from the Massachusetts Institute of Technology in 1890. Upon graduation she entered the competition for the Woman's Building at the Columbian Exposition. She worked within the classical style which was required by the Exposition Committee headed by Mr. Burnham, architect. This very young woman had to contend with limited budget, bureaucratic red-tape, and an uncooperative Committee; she accomplished her goal but with severe mental stress to herself. Ms. Hayden recovered her health, but the remainder of her career is unknown.

entered architecture and related fields. Consequently, all of these groups become dormant — except one chapter of the AWA in Los Angeles, California.

Within the last five years, discussion among women in architecture and related disciplines has again increased. Today new groups have developed in Boston, New York, and elsewhere to examine how professional objectives and procedures should be revised. Women members of The American Institute of Architects have organized into an identifiable pressure group, and in 1963 the International Union of Women Architects held its first congress in Paris. A weekend seminar, Women In Architecture, was held in January 1972 at the Virginia Polytechnic Institute and State University. The Open Design Office and Women's Design Center Inc., a non-profit corporation, was founded by five women in Cambridge, Massachusetts, to practice, research, and promote the role of women in the environmental professions. In Boston, WALAP (Women Architects, Landscape Architects, and Planners) studied the problem of serious part-time work for women and presented their findings in the *Architectural Forum* of September 1972. In New York, the Alliance of Women in Architecture has investigated discrimination within the profession, and has formed the Licensing Support Activity to help women obtain professional registration. Through activities of this kind women have begun to re-evaluate their function within the profession and also the function of architecture within our nation. Of course, the possibility exists that women will continue to isolate themselves within their own female groups, but hopefully these separatist tendencies represent a transition period giving female professional architects time to gain confidence while experimenting with alternative methods of architectural practice which the profession in general may in time adopt.

These suggestions depend on what direction American women, and women architects, decide to take from here. Will more women join those few who are now practicing architecture? Will women take a greater role in trying to resolve the problems — social, material, ecological — pertaining to the physical development of our nation? Will women participate in redefining the objectives of architecture and so make it more responsive to society's needs? It would be foolish to make predictions for the future, for it is the women architects, and those women interested in entering the profession, who will determine the outcome of these and other issues — but the history of women in architecture suggests that the precedents of social concern will remain dominant in their goals.

To think, however, that all women architects agree with each other, or that they did in the past, is ridiculous; to think that there are "male" and "female" goals in architecture is, perhaps, just as naive. But that is not to say that women do not bring with them different attitudes, experiences, and values to the practice of architecture. If there is one real difference between male and female architects in their professional practice, it is the pertinent one of specialization. In current office practice there is now a tendency to specialize in one phase — design, administration, production, etc. — but in their history women architects have resisted specialization. Their approach to the profession encompasses many interrelated aspects and facets of knowledge. Flexibility and resourcefulness have been their social conditions and have prepared them to seek variety in their work. Though diversity might be counter to present office practice, it is definitely not contrary to architectural traditions, nor to the future development of the profession. The diversity found within each woman architect's career is, in a sense, her strength for meeting the complex needs of our society in the future.

Hopefully, more women will enter architecture; but this doesn't mean that suddenly, with an increase of females, the profession will find solutions for all our environmental ills. Whether expectations will be set too high or too low, the American woman architect now must deal with the rights she has finally won. One woman whose architectural career spanned two world wars and the great depression stated it so well when she wrote to me that the recognition of women "is now developing rapidly, too late to do me much good, but I rejoice to see it coming. I just hope that women will be able to handle it now that they are getting it. That will not be easy to do." [16]

Unfortunately, women in the architectural profession are not immune to general conditions in society that have been adverse to all women professionals and working women. Architecture is not the exception, but follows the rule of low representation of women in high status jobs and the professions. In the United States women constitute only 22 percent of the faculty in institutions of higher education, 9 percent of the scientists, 7 percent of the physicians, 3 percent of the lawyers, and 1 percent of the engineers.[17] Architecture ranks with engineering in having less than a 2 percent representation of women.

House in Dover, Massachusetts, heated with solar energy, by Eleanor Raymond and Dr. Maria Telkes, 1948.

In 1970 there were 31 million working women who supplied this country with 38 percent of its workers. It is evident from such statistics that, though women make up nearly two-fifths of the work force, they do not begin to reach their expected representation in top-level positions, and certainly not in architecture. Though people might want to believe that the status of women has improved over the years, it is simply not true. In fact, history points the other way: "occupationally women are more disadvantaged, compared with men, than they were 30 years ago."[18]

Not only are women doing poorly in the public arena, but they have lost jobs in the domestic domain as well through decrease in family size and the relative drop in level of skills required for domestic responsibilities. The domestic role for American women has shrunk in every direction. The United States Department of Labor reports that for most women "homemaking is no longer a full-time job";[19] it finds that even for women who have children, and do not work while their children are young, there still remains a period of twenty-five years or more of working life expectancy. The nineteenth-century "corporation" that included maiden aunts, uncles, grandparents, children, parents, and servants, has been drastically cut down, if not dissolved. American women, who were once the executive directors of these family "corporations," have indeed lost a lot with the loss of their former domains, for these provided not only status but occupations. Consequently, women today, particularly those who are educated and otherwise secure, have become almost outsiders in the present organization of society. Men make a life of work and comradeship within their offices; children and teenagers have their schools and schoolmates. Women, on the other hand, are employed as homemakers for a few years and then are left with twenty-five years of free time.

For many women, however, there are no years of "free time," for they must enter the labor force early and remain in it until retirement age to earn money to support themselves and their families. It is startling to find that 70 percent of America's working women fall into this category; these women are single, widowed, divorced, separated, or have husbands who earn less that $7,000 a year. Half of these women have a pressing economic need, while the other half work to provide their families with more than the bare essentials.[20] To these women their earning power is extremely critical, yet they are the very ones, hampered by little education, poor training, and few opportunities for advancement, who hold the most menial positions.

Only 30 percent of all working women have husbands who earn more than $7,000 a year; it is women who do not have an economic need who generally do not work. One might like to believe that the educated woman, whose husband is financially secure, uses her education to improve the conditions of her community and nation. Sometimes this is the case, especially with volunteer work, but it is rarely true in the professions, social services, and business. The inability to find competent child-care professionals and, most important, the refusal of many fathers to share equally in the time-consuming child-rearing process prohibits women with young children from pursuing careers. But even when the children reach school age, the woman by volition, social conditioning, and often pressure from her husband, remains confined to her house, which is no longer a domain. For women trained in architecture, it means that few are practicing their profession and that many are wasting their skills and years of education. Granted, it is difficult to start a career at age forty, but between the ages of forty and sixty-five there are still twenty-five potentially productive years. Unfortunately, like other women who have gained security, the woman trained in architecture often joins the idle, being supported privately by her husband and publicly by her nation.

But existing educational and related job opportunities are helping to push many women out of the public domain and into the domestic. Unfortunately, few women are receiving the kind of education which leads to practicing a profession. "In spite of the rising number of women entering and graduating from institutions of higher education, the disparity in the proportion of higher degrees earned by women and men today is as great as or greater than it was in 1930. Women earned 38 percent of all degrees conferred in 1966, as compared with 40 percent in 1930." [21] This decrease in the proportion of higher degrees earned by women applies to architecture as much as to the other professions. There was a higher percentage of women receiving architectural degrees in the 1940s than there is today.[22] When the Cambridge School closed in 1942, Henry Frost believed that women had finally achieved equality of admission to professional architectural schools. He and others misread the progressive trend at that time and assumed that female admissions would continue to increase even after the men had returned from the Second World

War. But when the men returned, they simply took back the places taken by women during their absence. Even the new schools that had been established over the years to meet the country's increases in population were predominantly male in their enrollment. Today some of the architectural schools claim that few women apply for admission, while others claim that they accept the same proportion of female as male applicants. But women are claiming discrimination and have presented enough evidence to make the United States government question admission policies of these professional schools. However true or false the claims and allegations turn out to be, the fact remains that very little effort is made by either the schools or society to recruit and encourage women to train for architecture.

Further, women looking at the job market do not find the same opportunities as men do. Though legislation has been passed by Federal and State governments to prevent discrimination in pay and employment, differences do still exist in all fields. The Women's Bureau of the United States Department of Labor admits that "the barriers are still high against employing women in professions other than those traditionally associated with women." [23] The profession of architecture is not traditionally associated with women, and so it is not surprising that female architects earn less than their male peers. The New York's Alliance for Women in Architecture conducted a survey resulting in the following statistics.

Of the males answering, the average (mean) income was $15,800. For the females, the average income was $13,200. When cross-correlated for income, experience, and sex, it was found that the "normal" male would begin work at $10,470 a year, out of college. Each year thereafter his salary woud increase $700. The normative female would begin at $8,740 a year, and have a salary increase each year of $573. [24]

The AWA report goes on to state that "the sample generally indicated little difference between the sexes on education and registration." In other words, training and education help little in a woman's income growth. Even more shocking and discouraging for all working women is the disclosure that the differential between men and women's salaries is greater now than it was ten to fifteen years ago. [25] Not only does a discrepancy exist in salaries, but it exists in job advancement. Women architects remain in the middle ranks, rarely becoming associates or partners — unless married to the boss. Even though holding a high position in her firm, one woman wrote that "I feel that it has taken me twice as long to progress in this profession as it would have taken if I were not female."[26]

Strong accusations of job discrimination have come from a vast variety of sources, but perhaps discrimination is a misleading term for the American woman's struggle today. She is, after all, fighting the after-image of conventional nineteenth-century society. Each act of "discrimination" is an attempt to impose nineteenth-century values on twentieth-century life situations. The division of the public realm and the domestic realm continues in the minds of twentieth-century men and women, even though it does not correspond to the reality of lives today. Men are holding on tenaciously to their dominion while some women are trying to magnify through myth and prejudice their shrunken domestic domain. Unequal education, lower pay, and slow job advancement for women are all reflections of this unhealthy attempt to keep in force a dying social structure.

As much as there is need to focus attention on the damage done to men and women both by perpetuating outdated notions of the past, there is the urgency to work on problems more related to the future. With population pressures, polluting industries, decaying cities, shrinking natural resources, and a growing national debt, there is no lack of tasks to be undertaken by capable and concerned women and men. In fact, the problems are serious enough that no man or woman can, when you think about it, justify idleness. Architecture, at its best, deals with these conditions in the physical and social environment, and hopefully architecture will play some part in their solution. It is this challenge which is perhaps the most compelling incentive for more women to enter the profession. The alternative of continuing their social isolation within the shrinking confines of the domestic domain becomes increasingly unhealthy. The national environment is woman's as it is man's, though it is perhaps distinctly her challenge to make the task of putting this "home" in order a shared one.

The profession of architecture, both as it is practiced and taught in schools, is re-evaluating its role in society. Increasingly today architects are trying to deal with the problems of the many rather than those of the few. Architecture, the most traditional of professions, is in the process of changing course. The inclination to serve only the corporate and individual elite with prestige buildings is slowly passing. With this change comes the corresponding challenge and need for women and men to work together on more general and at the same time more stringent environmental problems. Their range and complexity have just begun to be explored, but even now, at the beginning, the need for interdisciplinary collaboration and for the inputs gained from a diversity of experience and training is obvious. This again indicates the valuable contribution that women architects could make.

Though both women and men professionals are discussing and re-evaluating the proper concerns of architecture, little will come of these efforts until they are implemented through office practice. Architecture is not made of words; architecture is not what is drawn on paper, but what is constructed into physical form to be used and lived in. The office is where this process occurs, where a philosophy (or lack of one) becomes translated into action as lines on paper become tangible structures. At this point in history there is little evidence in office practice that supports new goals or ideas and little indication, either, that future office practice will be much different.

For example, the typical office organization impedes the introduction of new or opposing points of view. The office structure is pyramidal in the delegation of authority, with one principal or a few partners at the top; next down are the associates, then the project managers, project captains, designers, and finally, an array of draftsmen under them. The office boys are at the bottom, with the secretaries placed to one side ranking with draftsmen in pay and authority. Each person in the organization, from principal to secretary, is vital to the success of any project, but this interdependency is not reflected in the typical office structure where principals and associates are the only permanent members of the firm. Project managers, job captains, designers, draftsmen, secretaries, and office boys seldom achieve permanent positions, and usually the turnover in their ranks is high. Promotion in the pyramidal structure is based upon managerial and administrative accomplishment rather than upon performance of direct architectural skills. Consequently, as an architect rises to the top of the pyramid, the administrative responsibilities increase and involvement directly with the architectural process is correspondingly diminished.

Each rank on the office pyramid has its defined duties, which vary only slightly from firm to firm. The principals decide the policies of the firm, oversee the work, and are responsible for gaining new commissions for the office. The associates help the principals in these duties and are responsible also for seeing that directives from the top are carried out by the staff. The project managers and job captains organize the individual projects, working directly with the clients, specification writer, cost consultants, governmental agencies, and regulatory boards. On smaller projects the job captain and designer are one and the same person, while on more complex projects the duties are divided. The draftsmen not only neatly render the sketches of others but work out the details that in the end greatly influence a building's aesthetic and functional character. The office boys are charged with running errands, making deliveries, building models, and other diverse tasks. The secretaries answer phones and type letters, organize reports, systematize files, gather presentations for prospective clients, and perform a variety of daily jobs. Each project in an office requires the assorted skills of these various people, and little progress can be made without them working supportively together.

There are, of course, firms that do not follow this structure. Some firms are small, limited to one or two principals, a secretary, and a few draftsmen; some firms include five or six architects, all as partners, with no draftsmen under them. But in general, when a firm reaches the size of twenty or more, the pyramidal structure begins to take shape. Moreover, it is the organization of larger firms which is the most crucial and threatening to the healthy growth of the architectural profession. As architectural projects grow in size and complexity, the offices which handle them grow with them. As it has become less and less feasible for this scale of work to be done by numbers of individual practitioners, large conglomerate firms have appeared offering clients inclusive services and package deals, and their employees, from architects to office boys, the pyramidal structure with its limited opportunities and specialized tasks.

The real power and authority in the corporate firm rests with the principal or partners. It is the principal who has the power to hire and fire; to make decisions; to determine salaries, pensions, and profit-sharing (if any); to decide policies and goals. Principals choose the associates, and no one becomes an associate — no matter what co-workers might think of him or her — without the approval of the principal. The system is based upon patronage: this unavoidably inhibits the expression of opposing views and eliminates as well any kind of experimentation or innovation contrary to the principal's wishes. Even the associates who are usually experienced and conscientious architects have little or no power in determining the firm's policy and goals. Associates may make suggestions, but if too many are unacceptable, they will soon find themselves either ignored and stripped of responsibilities or asked to leave the firm.

Not only is this system based upon patronage, but it does not often reflect or represent the inputs of the staff. Rarely are the secretaries, even those charged with executive responsibility, included among the associates. The architects who actually design the buildings are also excluded from decision-making unless they are willing to give most of their time to administrative matters. And certainly, one is not likely to find associates elected by the staff to represent their interests. In a nation that professes democratic procedures and representational government, the structure of the modern architectural office is a contradiction, to say the least.

The pyramidal office structure is detrimental to all people involved from principal to office boy, and because it is at present so pervasive, it becomes a regressive influence on the entire architectural profession. Surrounded by underlings understandably reluctant to give their candid opinions, the architect-principal of today's corporate firm is isolated from other firms by professional rivalry and from his staff by his very authority; he stands alone, with perfunctory contacts with his hierarchical staff, including younger professionals. What is far more serious in long-term thinking about the architectural profession is that if the office structure does not allow for experimentation, younger professionals will not learn their craft and art sufficiently to take their place in the future as leaders. Under the present system, by the time the associates and other young architects have won authority within the offices their minds are old and biased by doubtful, often erroneous, assumptions.

Both women and men architects are confronted today with this choice: they can continue to support, by becoming part of, the office pyramids until the architectural profession is so weakened in purpose that it loses its value to society. (And this has already begun to happen.) Or they can attempt the difficult alternative of restructuring the profession, schools, and office structures alike, to make the profession more responsive to both its own constituents and the diverse client groups in society. Historically, the American woman is conditioned for this role, having been since pioneer days charged with the physical and moral wellbeing of her family and nation. Each new wave of struggle for women's rights — voting, temperance, labor laws — has been directed towards the goal of bettering the general human condition. Hopefully women architects will seek no lesser goal in joining with their male colleagues to bring new life to the practice of architecture.

Footnotes

1. *Architectural Record,* "A Thousand Women in Architecture," Part II, June 1948
2. Ibid
3. Information was obtained by Doris Cole through her correspondence with women architects.
4. U. S. Department of Labor, Women's Bureau, "Background Facts On Women Workers in the United States," 1970, p. 1
5. Information was obtained by Doris Cole through her correspondence with women architects.
6. These statistics were obtained from the state Rosters available in 1971.
7. Letter to Doris Cole from a woman architect.
8. Letters to Doris Cole from woman architects.
9. *Time,* "Personality, Miss Luscomb Takes a Stand," April 26, 1971, p. 20
10. Information was obtained by Doris Cole through her correspondence and interviews with women architects.
11. Letter to Doris Cole from a woman architect.
12. Charles W. Ferguson, *The Male Attitude* (Boston, Little, Brown and Company, 1966), p. 242
13. John D. Kysela, "Mary Cassatt's Mystery Mural and the World's Fair of 1893" *The Art Quarterly,* Volume XXIX #2, 1966
14. "History of the Woman's Architectural Club, Chicago Chapter," 1933 from Bertha Yerex Whitman collection
15. "Association of Women in Architecture," 1973, from Lorraine Rudoff
16. Letter to Doris Cole from a woman architect.
17. U. S. Department of Labor, Women's Bureau, "Fact Sheet on Women in Professional and Technical Positions," 1968, p. 2
18. U. S. Department of Labor, Women's Bureau, "Underutilization of Women Workers," 1971, p. iv
19. U. S. Department of Labor, Women's Bureau, "The Myth and the Reality," 1971, p. 1
20. U. S. Department of Labor, Women's Bureau, "Women Workers Today," 1970, p. 4
21. U. S. Department of Labor, Women's Bureau, "Fact Sheet on Women in Professional and Technical Position," op. cit., p. 4
22. Statistics compiled with information received from certified architectural schools in the United States.
23. U. S. Department of Labor, Women's Bureau, "Underutilization of Women Workers," op. cit., p. iv

24. *The Architectural Forum,* "Rights Between the Sexes," April 1973 p. 71
25. U. S. Department of Labor, Women's Bureau, "Fact Sheet on the Earning Gap," 1971, p. 1
26. Letter to Doris Cole from a woman architect.

Bibliography

"A Thousand Women in Architecture," part II, *Architectural Record*, June 1948

Abell, Mrs. L. G., *Woman In Her Various Relations* containing practical rules for American females (New York, R. T. Young, Publisher, 1853) Schlesinger Library

Adams, John R., *Harriet Beecher Stowe* (New York, Twayne Publishers, Inc., 1963)

American Academy of Arts and Sciences, *Daedalus*, The Woman In America, Spring, 1964

Andrews, Edward Deming, *The People Called Shakers* (New York, Oxford University Press, 1953)

Beecher, Catherine E., and Stowe, Harriet Beecher, *The American Woman's Home* or Principles of Domestic Science (New York, J. B. Ford and Company, 1869) Schlesinger Library

Beecher, Catherine, *Miss Beecher's Housekeeper and Healthkeeper* (New York, Harper and Brothers, Publishers, 1873) Schlesinger Library

Beecher, Catherine, *The New Housekeeper's Manual* (New York, J. B. Ford and Company, 1874) Schlesinger Library

Billington, Ray Allen, *America's Frontier Heritage* (New York, Holt, Rinehart and Winston, 1966)

Bradford, Gamaliel, *Portraits of American Woman* (Boston and New York, Houghton Mifflin Company, The Riverside Press Cambridge, 1919)

Carey, M., *Practical Rules for the Promotion of Domestic Happiness* (Philadelphia, 1838) Schlesinger Library

Cleveland, Rose E., *The Social Mirror* (St. Louis, Missouri, L. W. Dicherson, 1888) Schlesinger Library

Current, William, and Scully, Vincent, *Pueblo Architecture of the Southwest* (Austin, University of Texas Press, 1971)

Dibdin, The Rev. T. F., *A Treatise on the Education of Daughters:* by Fenelon, Arch-Bishop of Cambray, Translated from French and adapted to English readers (Boston, Charles Ewer, 1821) Schlesinger Library

Dinerman, Beatrice, "Woman in Architecture," *The Architectural Forum,* December 1969.

Eggan, Fred, *Social Organization of the Western Pueblos* (Chicago, The University of Chicago Press, 1950)

Encyclopaedia Britannica (Chicago, Encyclopaedia Britannica, Inc., William Benton, Publisher, 1962)

Ferguson, Charles W., *The Male Attitude* (Boston, Little Brown and Company, 1966)

Frost, Henry Atherton, autobiographical manuscript — unpublished 1943 (William A. Frost and Henry A. Frost, Jr.)

Frost, Henry Atherton, and Sears, William R., *Women in Architecture and Landscape Architecture,* A Study for the Institute for Co-ordination of Women Interests, Publication #7, introduction by Ethel Howes (Northampton, Mass. Smith College, 1928)

Gardner, E. C., *Illustrated Homes:* a series of papers describing real houses and real people (Boston, James R. Osgood & Co., 1875) Schlesinger Library

Greenwood, Grace, *Stories and Sights of France and Italy* (Boston, Ticknor and Fields, 1867) Schlesinger Library

Hale, Mrs., *Manners* or Happy Homes & Good Society (Boston, J. E. Tilton & Co., 1868) Schlesinger Library

Hall, Florence Howe, *Social Customs* (Boston, Estes and Lauriat, 1887) Schlesinger Library

Harris, Neil, *The Artist In American Society* The Formative Years 1790-1860 (New York, George Braziller, Inc., 1966)

Hartley, Florence, *The Ladies' Book of Etiquette and Manual of Politeness* (Boston, J. S. Locke and Co., 1876)

A Lady, *The Young Lady's Friend* (Boston, American Stationers' Company, John B. Russell, 1837) Schlesinger Library

A Lady, *The Lady's Companion* or Sketches of Life, Manners, & Morals at the present day (Philadelphia, H. C. Peck & Theo. Bliss, 1852) Schlesinger Library

Laubin, Reginald and Gladys, *The Indian Tipi, Its History, Construction and Use* (Norman, University of Oklahoma Press, 1957)

Marriott, Alice, and Rachlin, Carol K., *American Epic: The Story of the American Indians* (New York, G. P. Putnam's Sons, 1961)

Meigs, Cornelia, *Jane Addams, Pioneers for Social Justice* (Boston, Little, Brown and Company, 1970)

Morse, Flo, *Yankee Communes,* Another American Way (New York, Harcourt Brace Jovanovich, Inc., 1971)

Nordhoff, Charles, *The Communist Societies of the United States* (New York, Harper and Brothers, Publishers, 1875)

O'Meara, Walter, *Daughters of the Country* (New York, Harcourt, Brace and World, Inc., 1968)

Patterson, Anne, "Woman Architects: Why So Few Of Them?", *Inland Architect,* December 1971

Radin, Paul, *The Story of the American Indians* (New York, Liveright Publishing Corporation, 1944)

Rambo, Ralph, *Lady of Mystery, Sarah Winchester*, 1967 San Jose Public Library

Rayne, Mrs. M. L., *Gems of Deportment* and Hints of Etiquette (Detroit, Mich., Tyler & Co. and R. D. S. Tyler & Co., 1881), Schlesinger Library

Reed, S. B., *House-Plans for Everybody* for village and country residences costing from $250 to $8,000 (New York, Orang Judd Company, 1878) Schlesinger Library

Rothery, Agnes, *Houses Virginians Have Loved* (New York, Rinehart and Company, 1954)

Schlesinger, Arthur M., *Learning How To Behave* A Historical Study of American Etiquette (New York, The MacMillan Company, 1946)

Sherwood, Mrs. John, *Manners and Social Usages* (New York, Harper and Brother, 1884) Schlesinger Library

Smith College Archives, Northampton, Mass., unpublished letters, records, and bulletins of The Cambridge School of Architecture and Landscape Architecture.

Sigourney, Mrs. L. H., *Letters To Young Ladies* (Hartford, William Watson, 1835) Schlesinger Library

Stowe, Harriet Beecher, *Household Papers and Stories* (Boston & New York, Houghton Mifflin Co., 1896) Schlesinger Library

Stubbs, Stanley A., *Birds-Eye View of the Pueblos* (Norman, University of Oklahoma Press, 1950)

The Family Book: or Instructions Concerning All the Relations of Life (New York, D. Appleton & Co., 1835) Schlesinger Library

The New York Times, "Fighting the System in the Male-Dominated Field of Architecture," Sunday, April 11, 1971

The New York Times, "What Is a Woman? Teen-agers Have Their Own Definitions," Thursday, May 6, 1971

The New York Times, "One Working Mother Versus the I.R.S.," May 20, 1971

The Right Hon. the Contess of ***, *Good Society* (London & New York, George Routledge & Sons, 1869) Schlesinger Library

Thornwell, Emily, *The Lady's Guide* to perfect gentility (New York, Derby and Jackson, 1856) Schlesinger Library

Trollope, Mrs. Frances, *Domestic Manners of the Americans* (New York, Alfred A. Knopf, 1949)

Tuthill, Mrs. Louisa C., *The Young Lady's Home* (Boston, William J. Reynolds and Co., 1847) Schlesinger Library

Ungers, Oswald and Liselotte, "Early Communes in the USA," A. D. Architectural Design 8 1972

Vaux, Calvert, *Villas and Cottages* (New York, Harper and Brothers, Publishers, 1857)

Ward, Mrs. H. O., *Sensible Etiquette* (Philadelphia, Porter and Coates, 1878) Schlesinger Library

Waters, Frank, *Book of the Hopi* (New York, Ballantine Books, 1970)

Wells, Kate Gannett, *About People* (Boston, James R. Osgood and Company, 1885) Schlesinger Library

Wharton, Edith, and Codman, Ogden, Jr., *The Decoration of Houses,* (New York, Charles Scribner's Sons, 1897)

Wheeler, Gervase, *Rural Homes* or sketches of houses suited to American country life with original plans, designs, etc. (Auburn, Alden Beardsly and Co. 1853) Schlesinger Library

Wright, Mrs. Julia McNair, *The Complete Home:* an Encyclopaedia of Domestic Life and Affairs (Philadelphia, Bradley, Garretson & Co., 1879) Schlesinger Library

Young, Agatha, *The Women and The Crisis, Women of the North in the Civil War* (New York, McDowell, Oblensky, 1959)

U. S. Department of Labor, Women's Bureau, "Underutilization of Women Workers," 1971 (revised)

U. S. Department of Labor, Women's Bureau, "Fact Sheet on Women in Professional and Technical Positions," November 1968, WB 69.60

U. S. Department of Labor, Women's Bureau, "Women Workers Today," June 1970 WB 70.211

U. S. Department of Labor, Women's Bureau, "The Myth and the Reality," April 1971

U. S. Department of Labor, Women's Bureau, "Background Facts on Women Workers in the United States," 1970 0-387-152

U. S. Department of Labor, Women's Bureau, "Facts About Women's Absenteeism and Labor Turnover," August 1969 0-361-490

U. S. Department of Labor, Women's Bureau, "Fact Sheet on the Earning Gap," February 1971 0-419-373

U. S. Department of Labor's Women's Bureau, "Profile of the Woman Worker," April 1970 WB 70-127

U. S. Department of Labor, Women's Bureau, "Changing Patterns of Women's Lives," 1970

U. S. Department of Labor, Women's Bureau, "Why Women Work," 1971 (revised)

i press series on the human environment

World of Variation
by Mary Otis Stevens and Thomas F. McNulty
cloth $6.95; paper $2.95

The Ideal Communist City
by Alexi Gutnov and other Soviet Planners and architects. Translated
from the Italian by Renee Watkins
cloth $6.95; paper $2.95

Playing Urban Games: The Systems Approach to Planning
by Martin Kuenzlen
cloth $6.95; paper $3.95

Towards a Non-Oppressive Environment
by Alexander Tzonis
cloth $6.95; paper $3.75

From Tipi to Skyscraper: a history of women in Architecture
cloth $8.95; paper $3.95

Struggle For Peace: Quebec, a study in the Ecology of Culture
by Marcel Bélanger and Melvin Charney
cloth $8.95; paper $4.25

T